ONE BITE AT A TIME

ONE BITE AT A TIME

HOW *EVERY* MANAGER
CAN USE SIX SIGMA TO
MAKE A DIFFERENCE

*

DAVID BREWSTER AND
GARY CALWELL

MONTEREY
PRESS

First Published in 2006
by Monterey Press
PO Box 319
Carlton North VIC 3054
Australia
www.monterey-press.com

Author contact: info@obaatime.com
Website: www.obaatime.com

Cover design by Nu-Image Design
Interior book design and typesetting by JustYourType.biz

National Library of Australia
Cataloguing-in-Publication entry

Brewster, David, 1965- .

One bite at a time : how every manager can use Six Sigma to make a
difference.

ISBN 0 9751474 1 2 (pbk.)

1. Management. 2. Six sigma (Quality control standard).
3. Organizational effectiveness. I. Calwell, Gary. II. Title.

658.401

For our daughters:

Laura, Megan, Matilda, Sarah,
Rosie and Emily

Acknowledgments

Firstly, we would like to acknowledge the efforts of the hundreds of participants who have taken part in programs using the *One Bite at a Time* approach. Their generous feedback, comments and suggestions helped shape *One Bite at a Time*. We are constantly inspired by what front-line staff and their leaders can do if they are simply given the opportunity.

To our clients who have had enough faith in the approach to let us loose on their employees. To our numerous friends, colleagues and family members who provided valuable feedback. To Heather Kelly for her mastery of the written word and for her many suggestions on how we could improve the prose.

And finally, to our wives, Judi and Karen, and our daughters for putting up with the weird and wonderful hours needed to pull a project like this together.

CONTENTS

Introduction

If you are a supervisor, team leader or manager and you're looking for ways to improve the quality and efficiency of your team's work, then this book is for you.

The *One Bite at a Time* approach has been used by thousands of people in organizations as diverse as a corporate bank and a regional hospital. These organizations have seen service improvements of over 50 per cent and productivity gains worth tens, and even hundreds, of thousands of dollars – identified and implemented by those who actually do the work. Whether you are a small-business owner, a supervisor in a large corporation or anything in between, if you have a team of people working for you, you can benefit from using this approach.

One Bite at a Time is based on Six Sigma, a very popular quality and management improvement methodology. Since it was developed at Motorola in the mid-1980s, Six Sigma has been used by many of the world's largest and most profitable companies, such as GE, DuPont, Ford and Honeywell. However, you don't have to be a multi-national corporation with a multi-million-dollar budget to benefit from Six Sigma.

One Bite at a Time removes the complexity that can surround large-scale Six Sigma programs. It combines the Six Sigma five-step improvement model with a few simple tools used in Six Sigma and elsewhere. The result is an easy but remarkably effective method for managers at all levels to use with their people to find better ways of doing their jobs.

It doesn't matter if you've never heard of Six Sigma: you'll learn all you need to know in this book. On the other hand, if you are familiar with Six Sigma, you'll notice that *One Bite at a Time* places much less emphasis on statistical analysis and is more focused on getting something done on a smaller scale in a relatively short time.

In the end, management is about getting the most out of your team. As you'll learn from this story, *One Bite at a Time* can help you do this in a simple yet powerful way.

Prelude:
THE CHALLENGE

chapter 1

As I approached my boss's office, I could see Amanda coming from it. Something seemed different. Her normally animated gait looked decidedly downbeat. Her head was bowed, her permanent grin replaced by a grimace. Before I could ask what the problem was, she had padded quickly past, not even noticing me. Hesitating, I knocked and opened my manager's door.

* * *

I was the first to arrive at the small Italian restaurant. The warm smell of garlic wafted out, drawing in hungry passers-by and giving the place the buzz of busyness. Soon after sitting down, I noticed Julia come in. She spotted me and her face broke into a broad smile as she weaved her way between the tables. My smile was less enthusiastic.

"I've got a big problem with my boss," I said as soon as she sat down.

"What *problem*, Nathan?" she asked.

I should have known.

"OK, the *opportunity* I have is to convince my boss he's an idiot and that he should resign for everyone's good," I said.

Julia smiled but didn't say anything, instead looking at me expectantly. Julia often found herself acting as a sounding board for my frustrations. After meeting at college many years ago, we had always managed to stay in touch. Over the years we had become business soul mates and had spent many hours discussing various management *opportunities*, as she insisted on calling them. She always seemed to know when I just had to let off some steam.

"Last week," I continued, "he announced that we have to increase our weekly volume of processed claims. Then yesterday he pulls me into his office and solemnly announces that there probably needs to be a restructure. Despite the fact that we are winning more and more work, he needs to find ways to cut overall costs. He's given me and the other two team leaders, Amanda and Aaron, three months to look at how our sections work and find ways to be more productive. If we can't come up with anything ourselves, he will simply force the situation by retrenching one of us, along with a number of our staff. Can you believe it? How can he expect us to increase our processing rates while constantly cutting staff? I need more people to help – not less. Especially since half my people have received little or no training."

Julia let me ramble on for 10 minutes. I explained how unfair I thought this ultimatum was. That my staff were already working plenty of overtime. That I wondered whether taking on this fight was really going to be worth it.

"Isn't Amanda due to get married in a few months?" recalled Julia.

"Yes," I said. "So you can imagine how this is stressing her out. Especially after her fiancé was cut back to part time last month. Then there are the three babies due in the next six months amongst my team's families, plus two other weddings. And the small issue of my own renovation that has to be paid for."

"Wow! And your boss accuses your team of not being productive," laughed Julia.

"Very funny," I said with a wry smile. "On top of all that, there's the fact that, as usual, Aaron is just not interested in working on this with Amanda and me. It's his way or no way for him. He just sees the downsizing as a *fait accompli*, so he'll do everything he can to make sure he wins what he sees as a competition between the three of us.

"So," I said finally, "do you still think this is an opportunity, not a problem?"

Julia was silent for a few moments. She is a middle manager like me; a team leader with a large bank. Just like me, she has struggled in the past to keep up with her workload and to meet her targets. With pressure from management and increasing customer complaints, she also found it difficult to keep up the morale of her team. However, I knew that her situation had dramatically changed since we had last caught up. She had been able to make some real changes that had improved her team's output, reduced complaints and seen morale skyrocket. I was hoping some of this might rub off onto me.

"There must be something else you can do to improve your productivity. There always is."

"I've thought about it," I said. "I've looked through all my various lists for ideas. There might be a few things. But we're all working too hard already. Everyone's putting in 110 per cent."

"I'm not talking about working *harder*," said Julia, looking at me seriously. "I'm talking about working *smarter*. How long did you say you have to get a result?"

"Only three months," I said, shaking my head. "It normally takes that long just to think about any substantial change in our organization."

"No – that's perfect!" she said suddenly.

chapter 2

I looked at Julia doubtfully, but a waiter was hovering and she was concentrating on the menu. After our orders had been taken, I asked her to explain her enthusiasm for my tight deadline.

"Last year," she said, "we had a big productivity push. The circumstances weren't quite as grim as yours – no one's head was on the block – but nevertheless, there was plenty of pressure to perform. We went through a program called *One Bite at a Time* and it made a big difference. And guess how long it took? Three months!"

"Okay," I said uncertainly. I was already thinking there was no way I would get any funds to run a new program in the next few months. But for the moment I kept this to myself.

"Have you heard of Six Sigma?" Julia asked.

"Well, I've seen lots of books about it in my favorite bookstore. But I can't say I know anything about it," I said.

"Yes there are lots of books on it," Julia agreed. "It's become a very popular business improvement methodology that can be used to improve processes, increase quality and cut costs."

"I know which one my boss would want it to be," I muttered.

Ignoring me, Julia continued. "Jack Welch, who was head of GE for 20 years, drove a Six Sigma program that reputedly saved the company $4.4 billion – as well as providing countless improvements in quality."

Julia explained that Six Sigma, when applied broadly across an organization, almost becomes a philosophy which guides the way the organization works and improves. At the other extreme, it can be seen as a highly detailed, statistical approach to doing business.

I nodded knowingly, although I really had no idea what Julia was talking about. So far, this Six Sigma thing sounded like everything and nothing.

Our meals arrived and as we ate, Julia went on to explain that the core of Six Sigma is a *process* for making improvements to a business. It draws on a large number of common and not-so-common tools – things like brainstorming and cause-and-effect diagrams – to facilitate this process. At one point I stopped her and explained that this all sounded good in theory, but I couldn't understand the need for it.

"Okay. Let me ask you a question. How do you currently make improvements to the way you work?" asked Julia pointedly.

"Well …," I said, a bit stumped, "when something needs fixing, we just get in and fix it, I guess."

"How do you know you have a problem that needs fixing in the first place?" she asked.

I chewed on the last mouthful of my meal as I thought about this apparently simple question. "To be frank, we're usually reacting to some crisis or other. A few weeks ago, there was a sudden increase in complaints about mail being delivered late, so I rang the mail room and gave them a blast."

"And did that fix the problem?" asked Julia.

"Not really. They spent some time looking into it, but they were finally convinced that nothing had changed in the way they were working. So I went down to Shared Services and discovered that a new clerical assistant had been putting external mail into an *internal* mail tray. Her mail was being sorted twice, which takes time."

Julia gave me the look of someone who has just been dealt a winning card. "That's a very small example, but a good one, of why programs like Six Sigma are necessary. Put simply, if we don't have a structured way of dealing with problems – big and small – we all have a tendency to jump to conclusions and to implement the first solution that pops into our heads. Often, that first solution isn't the right one but we waste our own time, and that of others, realizing that.

"Six Sigma gives us a way to avoid doing that. The Six Sigma *process* makes sure that we invest our problem-solving energy in solutions that are likely to work – not solutions that *might* work if we're lucky."

As the waiter cleared our plates, I thought about this. It did seem to make some sense. I could think of a number of big investments my company had made in activities that were supposed to solve a problem, but which ended up being a waste of time and money. One infamous example involved over $200,000 being spent to overcome an assumed lack of understanding, by some customers, of our online services. A CD-ROM was produced to show them how easy and beneficial online account administration could be. However, it turned out that most of the customers who avoided the Internet did so because they didn't have a computer and knew nothing about using one – let alone a CD-ROM. Clearly an approach like the Six Sigma one Julia was describing would have identified this issue before the CDs had been produced.

After we ordered coffee, I had a sudden thought. "You've been talking about Six Sigma," I said, "but earlier you were talking about something called *One Bite at a Time*. What's the link?"

"*One Bite at a Time* is based on the principles of Six Sigma," replied Julia. "In a way it's a trimmed-down version of Six Sigma. Importantly, while Six Sigma is largely a top-down program that aims for large-scale improvement in big projects, *One Bite at a Time* is essentially a bottom-up approach, with a much more local emphasis."

Julia went on to explain that *One Bite at a Time* was developed to give front-line teams the opportunity to quickly but methodically identify and measure their own problems, to find the causes of those problems themselves and to implement their own solutions. "In our section we have about 120 employees including 10 team leaders. Within two weeks we had identified a range of small improvements – we called them 'quick wins'. Then, within three months, each team leader – all 10 of us – had completed a more significant project and made some real differences to our areas.

"The *One Bite at a Time* approach also gave me and my staff an ideal learning opportunity. Since the projects were smaller, the stakes weren't as high. The other team leaders and I could practice Six Sigma techniques, knowing that if we made a mistake, the consequences wouldn't be too dire."

Finally, Julia told me how the biggest thing that had happened since her *One Bite at a Time* experience was a dramatic cultural shift. "This was something we never really anticipated. Everyone is working much more as a team now. And instead of complaining about things but not doing anything about them, everyone has become much more proactive. They don't look to me to solve all their problems for them any more."

"Well it sounds like the program has really worked for you," I said, taking the opportunity to jump in as Julia paused for breath. "But your circumstances were a bit different. You had the luxury of learning from your experience; we're going to live or die by ours."

"True," replied Julia, "but the way I see it, you have to do something. So you might as well do something that has a better chance of succeeding and of delivering a better result."

I had to agree with that. It was all or nothing for us. So when, as we readied ourselves to leave, Julia offered to coach me through the *One Bite at a Time* approach, I could hardly say no. We agreed to meet at my place on the weekend and get started.

As Julia started to walk back to her car, I called after her: "Would you mind if I invited my colleagues?"

"That's fine," she said with her trademark smile. "The more the merrier!"

As I walked home I was feeling much more positive about the challenge ahead. But that feeling didn't last very long.

chapter 3

That night, curiosity got the better of me and I was up late browsing the Internet and reading more about Six Sigma. There were hundreds of websites and a seemingly endless supply of information to read. I soon realized that a whole industry centered on this management method. There were books, training programs, online forums and consultants. There were also online glossaries and dictionaries and links to all sorts of tools and software.

Julia had made Six Sigma seem straightforward. The message I was getting from the Internet was the opposite. In particular I read about various hurdles that can impede Six Sigma success and felt like I had each one of them in front of me.

For a start, there was a lot of emphasis on 'top management support'. All the case studies seemed to be of large companies with charismatic leaders - like GE, which Julia had mentioned. I read about GE CEO Jack Welch's carrot and stick approach. Any of the key executives who weren't able to or weren't prepared to support the program were simply asked to leave. Those who stayed were given significant financial rewards for embracing the program. For example, Jack brought in a rule that only managers with Six Sigma black belts were eligible for stock options. Even with these incentives, Jack admitted that it still took three years to get all the senior staff committed to the Six Sigma culture. Now, while I certainly had a demanding manager, he was hardly charismatic and I knew there was no way he was going to actively support any new initiative at the moment. And my timeline was a lot shorter than three years.

Then there was the training that was needed to make Six Sigma work. There were 'green belt' training programs involving a week of full-time study. Beyond that there were 'black belt' programs involving up to four weeks of full-time study. What's more, it became clear that black belts were people who would typically be involved full-time on Six Sigma projects; green belts were involved part time. I couldn't afford any training, let alone all of this.

And then there was the jargon that had to be understood. Apart from black belts, there were master black belts and champions. There were DMAIC, DFSS and DMADV. There were binomial distributions, hypergeometric distributions and F distributions. There were toll-gates, correlation coefficients, sigma levels, multiple regression analysis, measurement system analysis, fractional factorials, factorial design, 5-why analysis and the

5S approach. This was a whole new language and I only had three months to be fluent in it.

It soon became clear how Jack Welch could easily have spent the reported $300 million in the first year of rolling out Six Sigma at GE. And why it would need someone with a personality like Jack's to make it happen.

It was easy to see how Six Sigma could be attractive to senior management. The huge cost-cutting achievements would capture any executive's attention. But would that interest last? Or would it become yet another passing fad? I could see it now: a launch with great fanfare, high initial enthusiasm and then, 12 months down the track, the program would be quietly cancelled, renamed or simply forgotten, replaced by whatever was in this year's best-selling management book. And in any case, I didn't have the time to convince them.

When my head finally hit the pillow that night, I'd lost much of the enthusiasm I had felt after lunch. Julia must have had more help than she was letting on.

* * *

"You're in the perfectionist's trap," was Julia's first response when I rang her the next morning to air my concerns. "I know, because I was there too. You want to be the best but doom yourself to fail by thinking everything needs to be done by the book. That's one of the dangers of reading about people like Jack Welch. It becomes too easy to make excuses like 'I can't do it because I'm not the CEO' or 'I don't have a billion-dollar budget.' Finally, you give up and achieve nothing – which, if I remember, isn't an option for you at the moment."

As Julia spoke, I began to see the wisdom in her words. Looking back over the last few years, I realized that I had done lots of reading and lots of dreaming but had not taken much action. I hadn't tackled the big issues because they were just too big. And I hadn't tackled the small issues because they seemed too insignificant to concern myself with. Instead, I'd buried myself in being busy, with only a crisis forcing me to lift my head. Yet I still wasn't convinced.

"But everything about Six Sigma seems BIG," I countered. "Big on money and big on time. I'm lucky to find the time to talk to my staff these days, let alone do any constructive work with them."

"Do you remember when you were a kid," Julia went on, "how your mother used to tell you to eat one bite at a time? Not to bite off more than you could easily chew and to finish each bite before starting the next? Well the same thing applies here. What we're talking about is using the essentials of the Six Sigma approach to digest each of our issues, but taking one small bite at a time. That's what we did: apply Six Sigma on a smaller, simpler scale – one bite at a time. And it worked well for us. The top-down, large-scale approach is only one way to gain benefits from Six Sigma. But you can also do it using a bottom-up approach that involves very little in the way of resources.

"Yes, in my case we were given some training. But only three days training spread over three months: hardly four weeks full-time. Other than the training, I was allowed one full day – also spread over three months – to work with all my staff on the project. I was also given some coaching support through the process. The rest of it was down to us. We had to fit our project work in between the rest of our work. But we did it. We did it because the process we went through allowed us to focus on making changes that we, as a group, wanted to make. That, in turn, provided the incentive for us to make it happen – despite the lack of time. I would have thought that in your case the incentive to stretch your-selves would be even greater."

I went to speak but Julia continued before I could get a word out.

"Sure, we didn't get benefits of the size Jack Welch can boast about. And it's true the really big Six Sigma savings come from really big, cross-functional projects – projects that cross numerous boundaries inside the organization. But remember, you haven't been asked to save the world in the next three months, just to make some improvements in your own department.

"I know you're as smart, if not smarter, than me. So if I can do this, you can too. The fact is, as I think about it now, my team and I did most of our learning as we worked on our project, rather than in the classroom."

There was silence on the end of the line for a moment before Julia went on.

"Look, I'm going to have to go. So I'll give you a choice," she said. "I can spend Saturday, as I've suggested, plus some more time in the coming weeks, teaching you what I've learnt about running a *One Bite at a Time* project. But I'll do it on one condition: that you commit to actually applying what you learn over these next few critical weeks. The alternative is that we have a nice quiet afternoon sitting in the sun, enjoying a few glasses of wine and reminiscing about our days at college. Bottom line: if you're not prepared to try this, I'm not prepared to teach you."

A pregnant pause. It took me a few minutes to absorb the implication of what Julia was suggesting. I hadn't banked on her taking such a hard line on this.

"And what about the time I need to spend with my

staff? I'm worried about how I can make that happen."
I said.

"Well that bit's up to you, my friend," she replied. "It
sounds to me as though your boss, for all his faults, has
given you the leeway to do what you can, however you
can, over these three months. So he shouldn't object to
you spending some planning time with your staff. I
know he can be difficult, but mostly that is because he
is caught between your needs and his responsibilities
further up the chain. In this case you aren't asking for
anything he doesn't have the authority to give you –
and you're making a commitment to see this through to
a finish. Surely he'll go with that?"

"I suppose you're right," I agreed. "When I think
about it, his unreasonableness is mostly about not having the power to say 'yes'. There's not much he can
object to with your suggestion, is there?"

Julia's mobile phone started ringing in the background. "Now I really do have to go," she said quickly.
"I'll see you on Saturday?"

I can't say I was entirely convinced yet, but with the
weekend only a couple of days away – and no better
ideas for dealing with my predicament – I couldn't see
that I had any choice. For a few moments I thought
about all Julia had said and it wasn't long before I started to feel positive about the challenge ahead.

I turned in my chair to share my new-found enthusiasm with Amanda, but found her bent over her desk, her head in her hands. She looked up, worry etched into her face.

"I've just found a resignation letter on my desk from my best analyst," she said. "He says he thinks morale around here is as low as it's ever been, and he just can't handle it any more."

We stared at each other blankly. My new-found gusto vanished as quickly as it had appeared.

chapter 4

When Julia bounced into my apartment on the Saturday morning, the contrast between her and Amanda was all too apparent. I had always admired both of these friends for their upbeat, positive approach to everything. Yet now Amanda could hardly muster an audible greeting when the two were introduced to each other. Julia glanced across at me with concern, but she continued getting herself ready, somehow managing to find just the right balance between compassion and enthusiasm.

"Didn't you say something about more than one colleague, Nathan?" she asked at one point.

Amanda and I gave each other a resigned look. "Yes," I replied. "Aaron decided he had something better to do, unfortunately."

"Oh well, that won't hold us up," said Julia cheerfully. Clearly nothing was going to get in the way of what she had in mind for us.

"In the spirit of *One Bite at a Time*," Julia started, "I'm not going to teach you everything you need to know today, just what you need to get started. Then, when you've put that into action, we'll do the next bit. Does that sound okay?"

We nodded.

For the benefit of Amanda, Julia went over the Six Sigma background she had already given me. Perhaps having learnt from her experience with me, she was careful to emphasize the difference between a large-scale Six Sigma project and the *One Bite at a Time* approach.

"What we will be focusing on is the Six Sigma *process*, which I mentioned earlier. We'll also work with a deliberately limited set of tools that you can use to apply that process quickly and easily," she said. "Sure, if you get deeper into Six Sigma later on, and you start taking on bigger projects, you'll probably need more tools – particularly statistical ones. But you can do a lot with a small toolkit to begin with. That's how you can keep it simple."

"So it's a bit like carpentry? I could start with a basic saw, hammer and screwdriver and work up to more sophisticated woodworking tools as my knowledge grows?" I suggested.

"Well I guess so," said Julia. "I don't know anything about carpentry. But the same applies to cooking, photography or any other hobby. You start by learning the principles and basic processes and use a small number of easy-to-use tools to start with. Then you slowly build on that as your experience grows."

"So what you're really saying," said Amanda suddenly, "is that for now, by following the basic Six Sigma *process* with a beginner's set of tools – we should be able to make some significant improvements in the limited time we have."

"Got it," said Julia, clearly pleased to see that Amanda was tuning in.

"In the end," she said finally, "it's not the tools you have that are important, it's what you do with them. So let's focus on the doing."

"So where do we start?" I asked.

"How about something to eat?" asked Julia.

"Oh, I guess we have to do that don't we," I said with a smile. "Give me a minute and lunch will be served."

As I put the lunch together, I started thinking about the challenge ahead. I suddenly felt that this could be a way to make a real difference to my department in a short time. I even started to think that maybe this challenge we had been set might turn out to be something positive. The sound of laughter suddenly swept through to me from the living room and it brought with it a sense of relief. It had taken the best of my coaxing abil-ity to convince Amanda to come today. If nothing else, I thought, at least she was being cheered up.

chapter **5**

While we ate our lunch, Julia gave us an overview of what the next few weeks would be like.

"What you're going to do is this," she said. "You'll each work with your own team to **define** a particular problem to work on. The 'one bite' that you'll be trying to chew. Then you'll go through a cycle of **measuring** and **analyzing** both the extent of the problem and its likely causes. Only after you've done both of those things will you take action to **improve** the situation and then put in place **control** mechanisms to ensure that the improvements stick. This five-step process, often abbreviated to DMAIC – one of those jargon words you came across, Nathan – lies at the heart of all Six Sigma projects."

"That all sounds a bit wordy," I said doubtfully.

"It did to me too, at the beginning," replied Julia, "but don't worry if it doesn't make much sense yet. To make it easier to digest and to do, we'll break the process up into four parts. Here they are," she said, handing us each a sheet of paper.

The One Bite at a Time Approach

1. First, with your team, **Define** a problem to work on.

2. (About 2 weeks later) **Measure** and **Analyze** the problem and possible causes.

3. (Another 2 weeks later) Make **Improvements** to minimize or even eliminate the problem and then put in some **Controls** to make sure they stay that way.

4. (About 5 or 6 weeks later again) Prepare and develop a presentation to your boss, and ideally some other senior managers, about your project and what you've achieved.

"Before you do each of these parts, we'll get together and I can explain what you need to do. That way you won't have to remember it all at once."

At this point Julia's words were only vaguely registering. As soon as I read that we had to give a presentation, I felt a tightening across my chest and a lump forming in my throat. I had imagined I would just do this across the boss's desk. Amanda looked across at me and knew exactly what I was thinking, because she knew I always got a host of 'fight or flight' stress symptoms whenever I had to get up in front of a group. I began to realize what a powerful motivator public speaking could be.

"Does all of that make sense?" asked Julia, jolting me back to reality.

"I think so," I said, letting the presentation issue go for the moment. "Rather than dump all the information on us in one go, you'll tell us how to do one part, then we'll each do it before you tell us how to do the next part?"

"Exactly. And, of course, along the way you can ring or email me with any questions that come up," said Julia reassuringly. "You too, Amanda. But before we dive into the detail, let's think about what you'll need to get started. In particular, you need to understand clearly the various roles that everyone will play."

* * *

As we cleared the plates, I thought I had better show Julia how much I had gleaned from all that information on the Internet.

"I've read a lot about the Six Sigma belts," I said. "Black belts, green belts, yellow belts, master black belts. Then there are the other roles like champions and sponsors. What do they all mean?"

"I'm not really sure myself," replied Julia. "They have something to do with the amount of formal education people have received, the number of tools they've been trained to use and the size of the projects they've worked on. In *One Bite at a Time* we didn't use any of those terms – nor hand out any belts. I suppose for a larger Six Sigma program you would need a more formal structure of roles, but for your projects you'll use just three."

Julia went on to explain that she would use the term *team members* to refer to the front-line staff who do the actual work. In our case, they were on the phones dealing with customers or processing the claim forms. She was pleased to hear that I had 12 direct reports and Amanda had 16.

"Those are good numbers," said Julia. "Some of my colleagues had nearly 50 direct reports. In the end we decided that project teams of no more than 20 would work best. In the bigger teams we made sure everyone was able to have some input though."

We were reminded that team members would still have to do their normal work during the project, as well as attend the occasional meeting to discuss their ideas. Team members should also be expected to help with doing some of the measurements, as well as playing other roles when we could let them.

The second group of people Julia specified were the *team leaders*. This was the role Julia had played and that Amanda and I would be playing. During the program we would continue to manage our own teams as usual. We would facilitate a series of team meetings where we would work on our improvement project with our staff.

"What's the third role?" I asked.

"*Management*," she said. She explained that in her case, the managers included her boss as well as the next level up. As *One Bite at a Time* was designed as a 'bottom-up' approach, management didn't need to have any direct involvement in the projects – in fact they were discouraged from doing so. However, management support was an important factor in determining the success of the program. Julia suggested it would be a good idea to invite our manager to introduce the program at the first team meeting. It would also be good to keep him in the loop if there needed to be any adjustments to rosters and that sort of thing.

"In our case," said Julia, "our manager even included our project in our performance appraisal system, which was in turn linked to our bonuses. You may not be able to convince your boss of that just yet. As a minimum, you need his tacit approval to try this. If you can get more than that – for example to have him launch your initiative, as I suggested – then all the better."

"I guess if we can have some success this first time, the boss will be more confident the second time around and might take more interest," Amanda ventured, amazing me that she could even look past the first project at this stage.

"Quite likely," replied Julia. "After all, if you and your team can make real improvements to your work without imposing on the boss very much, he could hardly object to that, could he?"

"So to summarize," I said, "you'll teach Amanda and me, as team leaders, about the program and what we need to do. Then it's up to us to get our manager's support and work with our team members on a project. Is that right?"

"Absolutely," Julia said, smiling. "I love the way you can summarize each part like that. If you do that in your team workshops, I'm sure your project will go really well."

As I was basking in Julia's praise, I noticed her staring out the window, deep in thought.

"What are you thinking?" I asked.

"Oh, I was just trying to remember back to the start of our very first project."

"Great," I said. "Hold those thoughts. I'll make some coffee and then you can tell us how to get started."

Over the next few hours, Julia took us step-by-step through what we would need to do to carry out the first part of the *One Bite at a Time* approach – the Define part – with our own teams. She seemed to cover a lot of ground, but when we looked at the six steps that were involved it didn't look too hard. Both Amanda and I had to admit that we thought we would be able to do it.

Stage One:
DEFINE

chapter 6

The following Monday I buried myself in the task of getting our *One Bite at a Time* program off the ground. There was no slack in the time available to us. It was exactly 12 weeks until P Day: the day our boss was expecting us to present our improvements.

I rounded up my team and told them about the situation. In the hurry of the previous week, they had been left in limbo a bit. They had the sense that something wasn't quite right, but I hadn't had a chance to tell them exactly what our situation was. Of course, this only led to the rumor mill winding up to full speed and, by the time we got together, they had convinced themselves we would be closing down altogether and their jobs would be moved offshore.

In a funny sort of way I think this helped me. When I brought them up to date, the news wasn't as bad as they had expected. I explained the challenge we were facing and what I proposed to do about it, briefly outlining the *One Bite at a Time* idea.

"This sounds like the usual stuff," said one of my staff at one stage. "Management create the problems, then leave us to fix them but without any resources to do so."

"Well, you can look at it that way if you like," I replied, "but a more positive approach would be to see this as an opportunity to do things our way. A big difference here is that we will identify what we think the issues are and we will decide which problem to work on. You have to agree that is different from having the corporate 'continuous improvement' people fly in, tell us what needs fixing and fly out again."

This created enough of an approving murmur from the team to indicate to me that they agreed, although no one was willing to say this out loud at this point.

"How are we going to find the time?" someone else asked. "We're already working overtime and ridiculous hours."

I felt I had no choice but to be completely honest about this. "Yes, I know it's going to be a challenge. And we might have to put in even more time in the short term. But the idea here is that we do it together, spreading the load. And the reality is that we don't really have a choice – we have to do something. The good part about this approach is that we'll be making sure that what we put our effort into *will* produce results. If we just act without thinking, we might fix something that wasn't broken in the first place, and we simply don't have time to waste doing that."

Another murmur of partial agreement. I couldn't help but feel I was doing quite well, considering I was basing my arguments entirely on theory at this point. I had no more real experience at this than any of my team.

In the end the group really didn't have a choice but to go along with me. We agreed to set aside the second half of the following Monday afternoon for our first meeting. Julia had told me this meeting might take as much as four hours, so I was glad when everyone said they would commit to staying until we had finished. In fact I was taken aback when two members of the group who weren't due to be on at that time said they would come in specially – on their own time.

* * *

When my 12 team members filed in for our first meeting, they surprised me by being quite animated, joking and talking amongst themselves. We were so busy and tightly resourced these days that it seemed just spending a few hours together for a meeting was going to be a novelty for them. I felt it was a good early sign that they hadn't wrapped themselves up in the negative idea that some of them could possibly lose their jobs.

Just as mine had, their eyes widened when they learnt that we had to present our project to management. Someone asked me who was going to present and for fun I told them that it was up to them to select a presenter. They responded with a chorus of "No way" as they shook their heads. I allayed their fears by saying that if no one else wanted to do it, I could present our project. It was Dutch courage though, because I wasn't feeling any better about it than they were.

After setting the scene again – much as I had done the day before – I told them that our task for this first day was to choose a *single* problem to work on in the coming weeks.

"Why just one?" came a voice from the back of the room. "We've got heaps of things to fix."

"That's true," I said, recalling having asked the same question of Julia, almost word for word. "But isn't it true that because we have so many things that need fixing, we end up not knowing where to start and, ultimately, doing none of it?"

"I have the same problem at home," said Trevor, one of our longest serving claim assessors. "There are so many things I need to fix on my house that when I get up every Sunday morning, I feel so overwhelmed just thinking about what needs doing that I give up – and go and play golf. My handicap's getting better though."

When the laughter died down I was able to go on. "That's a great example, Trevor. In one case, your house, you see the problem as way too big and so do nothing. In the other case, your golf game, you have, without realizing it, been slowly but steadily improving it in small increments – one bite at a time. No one would expect to become a professional-standard golfer with one quick fix. Nor can we expect to make our department problem-free straight away. But if we find something significant but 'chewable' to tackle first, we'll at least be heading in the right direction.

"We will identify lots of issues and problems today. Let me assure you that the ones that don't get selected to be dealt with now won't be forgotten – we will record them to look at down the track. But for now, we need to focus on taking just *one* bite." I took a mental note to make sure I documented everything we did during the day.

With no further questions being thrown up, I decided to get into the first of the six steps that Julia had shown me how to do.

The Define Stage

1. Understanding what we do
2. Customer Expectations
3. Brainstorming
4. Affinity Diagram
5. Shortlisting
6. Decision Making

chapter 7

Understanding What We Do

The very first thing we had to do was to answer, as a group, an apparently simple question: "What do we do?" When Julia had described this step it had sounded trivial and ridiculously easy, but it ended up taking quite a while.

I couldn't believe there were so many different opinions in my team. One person said we processed personal claims, another said we helped customers choose the best insurance product and another that we minimized revenue loss for the company. Now it's true that our team does all these things, but different people seemed to have different ideas about what was the most important aspect of our work. It was fascinating for me to realize how these different points of view would obviously affect the consistency of our decision making. It explained in part why some people, with a focus on accurate paperwork, would sometimes get fairly pointed with customers, while others seemed to spend all day chatting to people and building relationships.

After spending a bit of time on this first question, which identified our 'outputs', we continued by trying to answer another apparently simple question: "Who do we do it for – who are our customers?"

Again, at first everyone was puzzled. Our customers are … our customers. What more was there to consider? However, I had learnt to press these issues and in this case prompt the team to think about groups of customers with potentially different needs. For example, we had personal and business customers; call-center customers we actually spoke to and Internet customers we seldom, if ever, spoke to; even brand-new customers who knew very little about us and long-term customers who knew our systems quite well. Once again we surprised ourselves looking at how much variety – and overlap – there was within our customer base.

I explained to the group that, to keep this manageable, we needed to focus on one particular group of customers. It didn't take long before we settled on all customers who called our call center, rather than Internet-only customers. We knew that these customers represented a large percentage of our work and that both they and we were frustrated – and made unproductive – by lots of red tape.

Having agreed on what we do (our output) and who we do it for (our customers), we continued to work on answering three more apparently simple questions:

- What are the main steps we follow to do what we do *(our process)*?

- What resources do we need to do it *(our inputs)*?

- Where do we get these resources from *(our suppliers)*?

Julia had explained that discussing these simple questions with my team would be an effective way of giving everyone a common, high-level view of what we do and how we fit into the bigger organizational picture – not just the part we are involved with. For example, two of my team members had no idea what happened to the claims after we loaded them into the system. By drawing up a simple flow diagram to answer the 'main steps' question, everyone could see what happened before and after their own work. They also started to understand the concept of 'internal' customers. Perhaps most importantly, I think this step highlighted the importance of our role – even though to an outsider it just looked like unglamorous data entry.

It would have been very easy to skip this step and get straight into the brainstorming of problems, which is what everyone really wanted to do. But I now realize that, had we done so, it would have been with a much narrower, and therefore less creative, overall perspective.

chapter **8**

Customer Expectations

Having got the 'Understanding What We Do' step under my belt, I was starting to feel a little more relaxed about leading this workshop. I was particularly pleased that people were starting to contribute. I'd been worried about what might happen if everyone just sat there and said nothing. It occurred to me that this was probably another reason for starting our meeting with some fairly straightforward questions.

Wanting to maintain the momentum, I moved the group straight into the second step of the first meeting: identifying our Customer Expectations. Julia had explained that understanding our customer expectations was an essential part of the process. It would help us focus on what was really important.

We started by discussing what we thought our customers expected of us. After about 15 minutes, we had a long list of customer expectations. The top five were:

- Having the phone answered promptly.

- Being put through to someone who can help *first* time.

- Being sent what is asked for (and not having to ring again to follow up).

- Having different product options clearly explained.

- Receiving a prompt acknowledgement and apology when a mistake is made, and having the mistake corrected quickly.

I pointed out to the group that our list was inherently limited. We were essentially drawing on our personal experience both as call-center customers ourselves (such as when we rang other organizations) and via the anecdotal feedback we received from customers every day. I mentioned that I had had a quick look to see if there was any more quantitative customer survey information available, but so far hadn't come up with anything.

"Is that a big problem?" asked one of the team.

"Well, it's not ideal I suppose, but we have to work within the constraints we have," I said, thankful that

I had earlier challenged Julia with this very same question. "If we had lots of time and money, we could do a comprehensive survey of all our various customer groups and get a much better understanding of their expectations. Unfortunately for us, we have neither time nor money: we need to get results quickly, with a minimum of analysis."

"What has all this got to do with selecting a problem?" asked Trevor pointedly. "I thought that was what we were here for, and the longer we're here, the more work we're going to have waiting for us when we go back out there."

"Good point, Trevor," I replied. "In fact flushing out all the potential problems is the next step. But I think you would all agree that these first two exercises have helped us broaden our thinking about the extent of what we do. And that's important because to get the best results we need to look at the whole of our challenge together – not at our individual challenges individually. We need to work on the problems of the team, not the problems of the cubicle.

"But anyway, your question is well timed because, having gained a better understanding of what we do, who our customers are and what they expect, we can now move on to talking about the things that get in the way of us delivering our service in the best way we can. We're going to do that with a good bit of old-fashioned brainstorming. But let's have a quick break first to clear our brains and stretch our legs. Just one thing: no one is to go back and check their email. We've just spent some time broadening everyone's thinking on what we do and what's important. The last thing we want you to do now is get distracted by the latest urgent email in your inbox."

chapter **9**

Brainstorming

"I'm sure I've heard of brainstorming before," said Monica, an intelligent young analyst, as we poured ourselves a coffee.

"I'm sure you would have," I said. "It's a very common technique for identifying issues and generating ideas. It's easy to do, too, which makes it attractive. Like many of the tools you'll use, brainstorming has been around for years – long before Six Sigma. That's one of the nice things about Six Sigma – you can essentially use any tool you like as long as it helps move you through the process."

"Really?" replied Monica. "That's good. So all those analytical tools I learnt at college may not go to waste?" As she wandered off, I could sense Monica's mind in motion as she started pondering the possibilities.

One thing that struck me in the break was that everyone seemed to be discussing the material we had covered in our workshop so far – not the problems of the day or even the guillotine hovering above our collective heads. Far from being nervous, I was now looking forward to the brainstorming session.

Back in the room, I briefly told everyone what we were going to do and what the brainstorming rules were. I asked for a couple of volunteers to come up and scribe for me, giving each a block of sticky notes on which to capture one issue per note. Then I wrote the key question up on the whiteboard: "What are the things that get in the way of us doing our job?"

And then there was silence.

I couldn't believe it. Out on the floor there was never any lack of complaining, backstabbing and blame-shifting. Now the team finally had the chance to talk freely about their concerns – and they had been warmed up. But they just sat there, mute, like cell phones whose batteries had suddenly gone flat.

After what seemed like a lifetime but was probably less than a minute, a few people slowly started to call out some of their issues. My scribes wrote these on their sticky notes and placed them randomly on the board. This trickle gathered momentum and within a few minutes became a torrent of issues, problems and ideas that threatened to inundate the poor scribes. Issues built on issues and quite quickly we had almost filled our whiteboard with sticky notes.

Of course there was some duplication amongst all this, and quite a few things suggested were of dubious relevance to the customer-service focus, but I understood that that didn't matter at this stage. This was a brain dump and future steps would help make sense of it all.

After about 30 minutes our flash flood had subsided as the generation of issues, ideas and problems dried up. I thanked everyone for their efforts and we all sat back and surveyed our handiwork, the whiteboard no longer visible under a swarm of yellow notes.

Eventually someone asked: "So now what do we do – how do we make sense of all this?"

"Good question," I said. "To do that we'll use a variation of another of the tools adopted by Six Sigma. It's called the Affinity Diagram."

chapter 10

Affinity Diagram

I hadn't heard of an Affinity Diagram before Julia told me about it, so I was a bit reticent about having to lead my group down this path. On top of that, while the previous steps almost ran by themselves, this next exercise was going to be a bit more complicated.

As Julia had described it, an Affinity Diagram is a way of grouping ideas that are similar to each other. We had to take all the ideas recorded during the brainstorming and sort, group, combine and filter them until we had something that made more sense.

It was no surprise that when I explained this to my team, the response was a dozen expressionless faces. I cast my mind back to one of the things Julia had said: "The important thing to remember when sorting your issues is that there is no single right answer." With 100 or more issues in front of us and 13 people in the room, each with their own ideas on how to sort them, this was going to be challenging.

Julia had told me that when she now does this exercise, she doesn't follow a rigid process. Instead, she uses some general principles and tries to 'go with the flow' and just do whatever seems to make the most sense at the time. With these thoughts in mind, I asked a few of my team to help me and we started to furiously move the notes around the board, trying different combinations.

Julia's first principle was to sort the ideas based on who the problem affects and in what way. We used our Customer Expectations to help us with this. For example, the expectation that the phone is answered promptly was put up as a heading for one group. We were then able to move issues like 'too many personal calls' and 'filing cabinet too far away' into that group.

Julia's second principle was to try and create even-sized groups. Some of our groups had only a few trivial issues in them and we were able to combine them with similar groups to form a larger one. Other groups had really big issues that would clearly take a lot of time and resources to fix. We looked through those issues to see if we could break the group into more manageable chunks.

I noticed Trevor was placing the issue 'forms' into one of the groups. "Wait a moment," I said. Julia's third principle had just come to mind. While we hadn't wanted to discuss the issues during the brainstorming, now that we were sorting them, it was important to clarify them and make them more specific. "Who raised this as an issue?"

"I did," replied Monica, a little defensively.

Realizing that my question might have seemed a little aggressive, I more gently asked what she had meant. "Is the issue that we run out of forms, that they are too hard to read or something else?" It turned out the customers weren't filling in certain forms properly. With this new information, we were able to put the issue into a more appropriate group.

There was another sticker that said 'We need more training'. When I pointed out that this was a solution, not a problem, I was howled down.

"What's wrong with solutions," a few of the team gasped. "I thought that's what we were trying to do. *Solve* problems to improve our work."

"You're right," I admitted. "We do want to solve problems. But not just yet; that comes in the Improve stage of DMAIC. Right now we are still at the Define stage. It might seem slow now, but doing it this way will save us time in the end, because we won't be working on problems that don't need solving in the first place. Nor will we be applying solutions that we haven't proved will actually make a real difference."

"This is getting confusing," said another voice. "Can

you explain the difference between a problem and a solution?"

"Okay, let's look more closely at this training issue", I said confidently. Once again I was pleased to be able to use the same example Julia had explained to me. I started by drawing again on her first principle: asking "Who does the problem affect and how?" I varied it slightly to focus more on the customer.

"First of all, let's be a bit more specific about what sort of training you need."

"Okay," ventured Trevor. "We need more training on how to use the system."

"How does lack of system training affect the customer?" I asked.

"Because some people are making too many errors on the claims screen."

"How do errors on the claims screen affect the customer?" I asked.

"When an error occurs, it delays processing of the claim," said another voice.

"Exactly," I said. "So the *problem* here is that claims are delayed. Training is one – and only one – potential *solution* to that problem."

I noticed a small smile start to form on Trevor's face. This was a moment of truth – and I was privileged to see it. The very instant the penny dropped. I remembered clearly when it had happened for me. Julia had patiently explained the difference between problems and solutions to me in several different ways. We seemed to be getting nowhere when, in a flash, everything clicked and the difference became obvious. I was pleased for Trevor, and a little proud that I had been able to bring him to this point myself.

Trevor took the 'We need more training' sticky note, added the words 'on claims screen' to it and moved it under the heading of 'Slow claims processing'. It was now grouped with 'Bugs in the system', 'Constant distractions' and 'Receiving the wrong information', amongst others.

"So 'more training' is still up there as something we should do," said someone, "so despite all this talk, we'll do it anyway, won't we?"

"Perhaps," I said. "If we later decide that it really is an appropriate solution to our problem. We don't have the time or money to invest in any 'solutions' unless we can prove they will have an impact on our problems. We'll be looking at that in the next stage of this process."

Looking around the room, there were a number of frowns and blank faces. "Look, don't worry if you don't get this problem/solution thing right away. It will come. It's one of the most important aspects of Six Sigma, though. And don't get me wrong – solving problems is a good thing."

With that, the team continued to sort through the rest of their sticky-note problems and categorize them under the various headings. Despite a controversy here and there, the job was finished more quickly than I had expected and we again stood back to admire our work.

All our notes were now neatly arranged into various groups. I quickly scanned the board and picked out one of the issues: 'Desk too dark'. Someone had complained that her desk was a bit dark later in the day and so she found it hard to work effectively. "Here's an example of something that we can fix straight away," I told the group. I asked the woman to buy a small desk lamp the next day and I would reimburse her. For six months she had suffered with this but never thought to ask about getting the situation fixed. There were a handful of other issues like that – we called them 'quick wins' – and I made a mental note to either do them myself or delegate them within the next few days. If the team could see some quick improvements, even small ones, I was sure that would help keep them motivated.

chapter 11

Shortlisting

"Okay, everyone. We're nearly done. We have only one more thing to do today," I said after a few minutes. "It's time for our Goldilocks exercise!"

Once again the team gave me one of those 'What's he talking about?' looks. But I was getting used to that by now so I forged ahead.

"We've sorted our hundred or so small problems into various groups. Each of these groups is now a potential project for us to tackle over the next 12 weeks. What we need to do now is decide which one to do."

"Aren't they all worth doing?" someone asked. "After all, our customers expect all these things to be fixed, don't they?"

"That's true," I agreed. "But remember that we need to do this *One Bite at a Time*. It's far better to make a big improvement in one small area than try and fix everything at once and then end up not fixing anything at all. Our challenge is to choose something that is big enough that it will convince the boss that we're serious about improving our productivity, but small enough that we can actually get the work done."

"Hence the Goldilocks thing," Monica cried. "We need a problem that's neither too hard nor too easy, but just right."

"I couldn't have put it better myself, Monica."

"So how do we make that decision?"

I was getting tired at this point and I had to force myself to concentrate. I remembered Julia saying to put aside the 'too hard' issues first – and that was enough to put me back on track.

"What we are going to do first," I told my team, "is to work out which of these potential projects are simply too hard for us to complete in the time available." I explained that anything that was outside our control, that would require a lot of resources or that would simply take too long to fix should be moved into the 'too hard' basket. For example, our 'Lack of an easily understandable product range' potential project would require decisions from marketing and head office, and we all knew the chances of making that happen in three months were very low.

Once we had the 'too hard' issues out of the way, we

could focus on classifying the remaining potential projects as 'too easy' or 'just right'.

I pointed to another heading that related to customers being passed quickly to the person who could help them. When we looked at the list of issues under that heading, they were mostly trivial. Things like having no organization chart and no team phone list. This was hardly a project that would give us a lot to boast about in three months. So it went into the 'too easy' basket.

We had started with nine potential projects and put three aside as 'too hard' and three aside as 'too easy'. That left us with three potential projects in the 'just right' category.

I looked at the list of steps Julia had left me with and found we had reached the end of it. With a sense of relief, I was able to tell everyone that we had finished all we needed to do. I explained that I would go away and do some more work on which of the three potential 'just right' projects was going to be the best for us to deal with now (though if I were honest I would have had to admit I didn't know how I was going to do this).

"What about all the other projects and problems? We don't want to just forget them do we?" asked Trevor.

"No, not at all," I said. "With some of the 'too easy' ones, I'm going to pull some of you together to tackle them separately. Then we'll have some extra things to brag about in a few weeks. The 'too hard' ones will have to wait. Assuming we come through this, I guess we'll revisit those down the track."

For a moment I couldn't understand why that last comment was greeted with dismay on the faces of a few of the staff. Then I realized what I'd said about 'if we come through this'. What a stupid thing to say. In one short sentence I'd managed to burst the balloon of positive energy that had built up during the afternoon.

"Look, guys, we've done a terrific afternoon's work. I'm convinced we *will* come through this if we work together to tackle one of these projects. So don't lose heart on me now."

Everyone did their best to give me a smile as they left, but I could tell many of those smiles were forced. Left alone in the room, I wandered across to the window and stared out into the gloom of the early evening. Suddenly my doubts resurfaced and I found myself battling to maintain my own positive energy. I hoped I was right. I hoped I could hold this team together and that we could come through.

chapter 12

Decision Making

"Julia, I need some help. The meeting went well - really well. But now I'm all mixed up again. When we finished at my place, we were at the end of the first meeting. We didn't cover how on earth I'm meant to choose between the 'just right' problems. And let me tell you that I'm really not feeling that confident at the moment. I feel like the pressure's right back on me. The team are waiting for me to take the lead, but I know they have expectations about which of the problems I will choose. And some of them are losing hope too …"

"Hang on, hang on," interrupted Julia. "Slow down."

I stayed silent on the end of the phone.

"I'm really pleased to hear your meeting went well, Nathan. I'm a little surprised you have the energy to deal with this tonight, but I guess you're in a hurry with all this. I'll be quick. Let's focus on this decision you have to make. It's easier than you think.

"First, you need to come to grips with the idea that you have the *right* to make the final call on this. Remember that you are a manager yourself. Making decisions is one of the things you're being paid to do. Also, because you are in that supervisory role, you have a broader perspective of who else might be affected by the decision you make, and how they might be affected. You're also in the best position to consult others – colleagues and your own manager for example – before making a decision. In my case, I knew it was important to get the views of my manager to ensure that the project we chose would be consistent with the business's broader objectives."

Not getting a response from me, Julia went on to encourage me to use my own discretion to make a final call on which of the three short-listed projects my team would pursue. "You've already consulted your team extensively, so they can hardly feel out of the loop. And don't forget they all agreed, by putting the short-listed projects into the 'just right' category, that they would be happy with any of those projects.

"You can overcomplicate this process," warned Julia finally. "In most cases there will be one project that stands out as an obvious choice."

We ended our call and I tried to reflect on what Julia had said. But exhaustion enveloped me and my brain refused to do any more thinking.

* * *

First thing the next morning I went straight to the boss's office. To my surprise he was there. What's more he welcomed me in. I explained what we'd been doing and he seemed genuinely impressed.

"You've done all this on your own? Organized the meeting, brought your team together and facilitated the whole thing? How did you manage to cover the phones?" These questions were asked with a sense of admiration – not the angst I'd been used to. In fact the whole conversation had a feel I wasn't used to. The problem was I couldn't work out whether the different attitude coming from the other side of the desk was one of new-found optimism or resigned acceptance. Nevertheless, I pushed ahead.

"I was able to get Amanda's group to cover the phones. We're doing the same for her this morning." I replied. The news that another team was doing the same thing prompted another look of surprise.

I explained that my team had come up with three potential projects and explained each of them to the boss. Julia was right. Even as I spoke there was one project that stood out from the other two as an obvious choice. It addressed the productivity issue we'd been challenged with while at the same time being true to the quality focus of Six Sigma. And I knew that if we could succeed, we would be making our own lives easier as well. Talk about a win-win-win situation. By the time I got to the end of my outline, rather than asking the boss's opinion I simply told him which one we intended to go with: *Reduce the time to process a routine (Category A) claim*. He agreed this seemed a sensible choice.

"Nathan," he said as I rose to leave. "What you're doing sounds good. But keep it moving, won't you. Don't spend too much time analyzing without action. I'm getting plenty of pressure from upstairs to demonstrate productivity gains quickly. It's all I can do to keep them to their original promise of giving me three months."

I nodded and walked to the door. "There's one other thing you should know," he said seriously. "Your colleague Aaron has taken a different approach to you and Amanda. Yesterday he sought approval from me to lay off three of his staff. I should warn you that when it comes to the crunch, the accountants at head office will often see straight cost cutting like that as a positive."

With that he turned his attention to his computer monitor.

chapter 13

It was the weekend after our first team workshops. Outside, the day was flat, grey and damp, which more or less reflected the mood Julia encountered when she came through the front door of Amanda's house.

"Oh, come on you two. It can't be that bad," she exclaimed.

I explained Aaron's cost-cutting exploits and the sense of urgency that had emanated from the boss earlier in the week. "I just feel like we need to *do* something. We've both identified projects to do with our teams now. Why can't we just get on and fix them?"

"We've put in an awful lot of effort so far," agreed Amanda, "and we've only got past the 'D' of your DMAIC process. Now the pressure is on to act and we still have four steps to go."

Julia gave us the smile of someone who had been through all this before. "Stick with it, the two of you. The other steps are much less involved than what we've covered already. Many of the next steps are repetitions of what you've done, though in slightly different forms. And you have to keep reminding yourselves that we're following this process for a purpose – to get you a better result in the end. In fact the situation with Aaron emphasizes the importance of having some *measurable* improvements to demonstrate at the end of this. You know how much senior managers love numbers. Clearly Aaron will have at least one 'cost saving' number to present, even if that's all he presents. You don't need to beat him, but you do need to demonstrate that you understand the importance of quantifying your efforts."

There was silence for a while as Amanda and I chewed over these words. I knew Julia was right, and I also knew that having started the *One Bite at a Time* process, we really had no choice now but to continue. A quick quizzical glance across at Amanda told me she was thinking exactly the same thing.

"Well I suppose we had better get on with it," I said, still, I suspect, sounding a little unconvinced.

"Okay," said Julia with purpose. "But first, you'd better tell me how your meetings went. Despite the glum looks this morning, I know Nathan was happy with his. How did yours go Amanda? Warts an' all, please. I want all the gory detail."

Over the next hour or so Julia grilled us in a thorough debriefing of our first meetings. We described the initial skepticism, the difficulty in finding a time to meet and the eventual willingness of some staff, once they knew this was a bit different, to come in on their own time or at least for extra hours. We told her how we had worked with our teams to cover each other's phones to make sure as many people as possible could get to the workshops. And we shared the fact that we had both found running our meetings very tiring.

Finally, Amanda commented on the enthusiasm of many of her staff to get on with things immediately, despite the concerns of some of their colleagues. "One of the real positives of the whole exercise was that the team were very keen to fix the 'too easy' problems straight away. What amused me was that the same people who had been complaining about not having enough time to even clean their desks now somehow managed to find time to tidy not only their own desks but the printer and photocopy area as well."

"That seems to be a common experience – at least it certainly was amongst our projects. It's amazing how much initiative can be held back by invisible barriers," commented Julia. Then she continued, "You've both done a fantastic job. I have to admit I didn't expect it to work that well for you, given the small amount of training and support you've had."

"Well you did say once that I was smart," I threw back with a smile. "And we did have a good teacher. But

I think on top of both those things, the whole process is supported by a healthy dose of common sense."

"That's certainly true," replied Julia. "In fact, Bill Smith, the inventor of Six Sigma, is said to have described it as no more than 'organized common sense'."

"Now, we'd better get on with the next step, hadn't we?" prompted Amanda.

"That would be lunch, wouldn't it?" asked Julia.

"Your stomach always did come first," I laughed.

Stage Two:

MEASURE AND ANALYZE

chapter 14

We enjoyed our lunch without trying to work at the same time, as Julia had assured us that today's 'training' session wouldn't be as long as the last one.

"During the Define stage, we had to learn quite a few new concepts and also break some bad habits – like the temptation to rush towards solutions without having a good understanding of the facts. However, now that you've defined your project I think you'll find it's a bit simpler. That's not to say there isn't still quite a lot of work to do, though."

"That's what we're afraid of," laughed Amanda.

More seriously, I asked, "Is that why we're combining the Measure and Analyze stages – to make them quicker to do?"

"Partly," she replied. "But there is another good reason for covering these two DMAIC stages together. During the measurement stage, you'll make lots of … um, well, *measurements* relating to your problem."

I smiled and said, "I'm with you so far."

"Such a supportive soul," exclaimed Julia. "Okay smarty pants, what do you think you'll do in the Analyze stage?"

"That's easy. Analyze stuff."

"And the *stuff* you'll analyze will be the measurements made in the previous stage," said Julia. "So here's the point I've been trying to make. If you spend time and energy making lots of measurements without any idea of how you are going to organize or display the results, you may forget to measure something really important. So in other words, it pays to work out *how* you are going to use the information *before* you collect it.

"As well as that, the measurement and analysis stages tend to be a bit iterative. In other words, as you do some analysis you may find something else to measure, and the new measurements may lend themselves to some different analysis, and so on."

"Sounds like we could spend a bit of time going around in circles," said Amanda.

"That's possible," replied Julia. "But I think one of the benefits of not having too many tools in the kitbag is that it helps you avoid overanalyzing everything. And since you have limited time available to you, as we did, you'll have to rely on the Pareto Principle."

"What's that?" I asked.

Julia explained that the Pareto Principle is also known as the 80/20 rule. It can be stated in various ways but generally suggests that 80 per cent of your results will come from 20 per cent of your effort. Applying the Pareto Principle to the Measure and Analyze stages, we could assume that we would get close to 80 per cent of the truth by doing only 20 per cent of the possible analysis. "The Pareto Principle is, by the way, another Six Sigma tool that was well worn long before Six Sigma came about – Pareto lived in the 19th century. The principle shouldn't be taken literally, but can help us with the occasional reality check."

"Okay, if the 80/20 rule will help speed things up a little, I'm all for it. So, next question is: *what* do we measure?" I asked.

"And *why*?" Amanda added.

"Very good – you're learning," she said. "Keep asking those 'why?' questions. They'll come in very handy during the analysis stage. For now you want to measure two things: the current extent of your problem and the relative impact of its potential causes."

And so the afternoon went on. By the middle of the afternoon, Julia had covered all she thought we needed to know to run another workshop. And despite our misgivings due to the pressure from our managers, Amanda and I had to admit that, having successfully navigated the first meeting, this second one sounded a lot easier.

chapter **15**

Measuring the Problem

Tuesday afternoon and I was back in front of my team. I could feel a mix of hesitation and expectation in the room. There had been plenty of pep talks and heart-to-hearts over the previous few days, so I decided to avoid any more fluffy stuff and move straight into what we had to do.

"Now that we've chosen a problem to target, it's important that we measure how big that problem is. We need to do this for two reasons. First we need to be sure that the problem is actually big enough to be doing something about."

"So in our case, that would mean finding out how long it currently takes to process a routine Category A claim, wouldn't it?" asked Monica. "Surely we already know that it's excessive – that's why we nominated it as a problem in the first place."

"We *think* it's excessive," I said, "but we don't really know for sure. We also don't know what our customers think of our service level. After all, it is really up to our customers to decide whether the processing time is too long. So we might need to do some customer satisfaction measurement too."

I told my team the story I had earlier shared with Julia about the CD-ROMs aiming to promote online services. The original assumption of the team had been that customers were lacking information, so they set out to provide some. After the debacle with the CD-ROMs, the group had gone back to their customers to find out what they really needed to help them use online services. The answer, somewhat counter-intuitively, was *less* information, not more.

"That's terrible!" someone called out. "What if we're halfway through our project and we find that we don't really have a project at all – at least not one worth pursuing. Imagine all the wasted effort."

"It wouldn't be good, obviously. But let's put this situation into perspective," I said, suppressing my own fear that we would follow such a path. "For a start, had this group been following our approach, they would have discovered their mistaken assumptions early in their project – not halfway through. More importantly, they would never have invested all that time and effort developing and distributing the CD-ROM in the first place, effectively fixing a problem that wasn't there to be fixed."

"I suppose. I just can't imagine what it would be like to stand up at our presentation and have nothing to say except that we had isolated a problem that we didn't need to fix."

When discussing this issue with Julia, she had made the point that although the *One Bite at a Time* approach was about improving quality and productivity, its other purpose was for everyone to learn the various tools and techniques that could be used to make those improvements. This learning component was just as important – perhaps more so – than the actual improvements because, once learnt, the tools could be used over and over again into the future. I didn't share this with my team as, in our situation, we really *did* need to make some improvement.

Mustering all the optimism I could find, I tried to reassure the team. "There is one thing I have learnt very clearly over the last few years: that those who make mistakes tend to learn more, in the end, than those who don't. I think this is highly unlikely, but if it does turn out that we are trying to fix a 'non-problem', we'll just have to refocus our energy – and the problem – based on what we've discovered. I'm sure it would add something to our presentation in the end, because we'd be able to talk about the extra lessons we had learnt."

A few of the group looked unconvinced, but we needed to keep moving.

"I said there were two reasons why we need to measure the extent of our problem. Over the next couple of months, leading right up to our presentation, we will be making some improvements that, hopefully, will reduce the average processing time for these claims. If we don't measure what the processing time is right now, before we make any changes, we won't be able to demonstrate our success at fixing it."

I was thankful when this point was greeted with general agreement, so we moved on to discussing how we could go about actually doing the measurement.

I had given this some thought earlier and so I told my team that, like many organizations, ours already captured an enormous amount of data. I had, in fact, asked our IT department and discovered that one part of our main system captured the times that claims were made and another part of the system captured the times that payments were made – effectively the final step for the routine claims we were focusing on. "All we have to do is download both sets of data into one spreadsheet and then we should be able to quickly determine the processing time for each claim."

"I'll do that," interrupted Monica. "But it sounds more like analysis – I thought we were still on measurement?"

"True. The line between measurement and analysis can be blurry," I said. "Strictly speaking, creating the spreadsheets and collecting the data is the measurement bit. After you've done that you'll have some fun playing with the spreadsheet to work out what all those rows of numbers are telling us. I assume you'll be happy to do that bit too, Monica?"

"You bet," she said eagerly.

chapter **16**

"Apart from the size of the problem, there is something else that we need to measure: the extent of the potential causes," I continued.

"What causes?" asked Trevor. "We haven't talked about causes yet."

"That, Trevor, is the main purpose of our getting together today."

I explained that we needed to select the most likely causes of our problem and to identify, from amongst them, those that were having the *biggest* impact on it. "This will allow us to target our limited time and resources at those major causes and yield us the biggest possible impact on our problem."

In return for this explanation I received universally blank faces. Eventually someone bleated, "Could you go over that again, please. It was a bit too fast for me."

Once again I found myself teetering on the edge of my own experience. After all, I hadn't done this before – I was reliant on what I'd learnt from Julia.

"I tell you what. Let's do an exercise and I think it will become clearer. First, though, let's go back a step," I said. "Let's revisit our project's aim:

Reduce the average time to process Category A claims to less than two days."

"You've added something to that problem," Monica interrupted. "You didn't have a number in there before."

"Well spotted," I said. "At some stage we are going to have to set ourselves a specific target. We probably won't be able to settle on this until we've measured the problem, but let's just imagine this as a target for now."

"Good idea," Monica replied. "It certainly makes it feel more real, I think." It was quickly becoming clear to me who would be getting one of the key number-crunching roles in this project.

"Now that that's clear, we need to do another brainstorming session. This time we're going to try to come up with as many possible causes of our problem – delayed claim processing – as we can. This brainstorm will be different from the first one. The idea this time is to get a lot more specific. Instead of just putting everything up randomly, we're going to use a 'cause and effect' diagram." I drew the skeleton of the diagram up on the whiteboard, just as Julia had shown me.

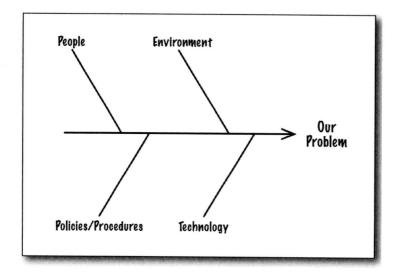

"It looks like a fish," said someone.

"That's right," I nodded. "In fact the cause and effect diagram is also called a fishbone diagram. It's another commonly used tool that is also used in Six Sigma. The idea of the cause and effect diagram is that it encourages you to dig ever deeper towards the real root causes of our problem. We'll use it in conjunction with another technique called '5-whys' analysis."

"Sounds like a group of religious men," said Trevor, causing a chuckle around the room.

"I guess so," I smiled. "Let me try and demonstrate as we start our diagram. Can someone give me one of the reasons why our claim processing time is longer than it should be?"

"Interruptions from the payout department," came the quick reply.

"Good," I said, "Now, *why* do they interrupt?"

"Because they need extra information."

"And *why* do they need the extra information?"

"Because we have access to it and they don't."

"And *why* don't they have access?" I asked, secretly pleased that this example was turning into such a good one.

"Because historically they've never needed it. Things have changed but no one has ever got around to applying for access. It has been easier to continue asking us."

I smiled. "So finally we get to the root cause of this apparently simple problem: the payout department can't quickly access the information they need to do their job. In this case, we have only needed four 'whys' to get there. The rule of thumb, I'm told, is that most often it shouldn't take any more than five 'whys' to get to the root cause."

"So it's a bit like finding the source of the noise

under the car's hood and fixing it there – rather than turning up the radio and hoping it will go away," said Trevor.

"Exactly," I cried. "You're on fire, Trevor. Can you all see how finding and addressing the root cause increases the chance that we will fix the real problem, rather than simply papering over it? We could fix the problem we've just worked on by providing the extra information upfront, in every case, but that would actually add to our workload, and it wouldn't fix the underlying problem. Talk about working harder, not smarter."

"Wouldn't asking 'why?' repeatedly get a bit tiresome all round," I was asked.

"I guess so, but as anyone who's had anything to do with young children knows, it's also the way we learn how things really work." I reminded the group of a time the previous year when we'd had some consultants in to review the way we were working. "On reflection, I think they relied almost entirely on the '5-whys' technique. That was how they got to the bottom of what was really going on. So now we need to do the same thing."

Over the next 30 minutes or so, we repeated what we'd done with the interruptions cause. Quite quickly, the team filled the diagram. It seemed the initial brainstorming exercise had lubricated their brains and the thoughts were now flowing freely.

Finally, someone said, "There seem to be a lot of causes for that one problem. No wonder we have a lot of delays."

"Not causes," I said, remembering another of Julia's mini-lectures. "These are all *potential* causes."

I explained this important distinction. "Remember the measurement issue we were talking about earlier. It applies here too: we shouldn't let our preconceptions cloud what's actually going on. So until we do some measurement, we can't be sure which of these potential *causes* is having any measurable *effect* on our problem."

"And the only way to find that out is to measure them too," said Monica triumphantly.

"Precisely."

I explained that we didn't have time to measure *every* potential cause. Once again, we used our collective 'gut-feel' to narrow the field. The group were quick to understand this and with a bit of discussion they quickly identified what they felt were the four most likely root causes of slow claim processing:

- Lack of clarity about what information is where.

- Lack of an effective fax filing system (leading to some faxes having lost pages).

- Too many exceptions to the rules (leading to escalated calls).

- Customers not completing their forms properly.

"Fantastic," I said. "Great job. Now we have five things to measure: our problem, plus these four potential causes. The final task for today is to work out ways to collect some data and make these measurements."

At this point we talked about measuring some of these things using more old-fashioned methods than the spreadsheet downloads we would use to measure our problem. This was important, as we knew that in all the terabytes of data stored on the company computers, there was unlikely to be anything that told us much about these potential causes.

The team agreed to set up a simple check sheet using a sheet of flip-chart paper posted on the wall near their workstations. The check sheet would have four columns, one for each of the potential causes. It would be up to every member of the team to record on that sheet – using a simple tick – every instance of one of these things occurring. So, for example, every time a fax had a missing page, they would record that. Every time a call was escalated due to a rule exception, that would be recorded. And so on.

I wrapped up our meeting by telling the group that, unlike the first stage, the real work in this second stage – the measurement and initial analysis – would take place back at our desks. Careful this time not to allude to potential disaster, I thanked the group and sent them off. I was tired – this facilitation thing used a lot of energy – but I also felt quite positive for the moment.

I walked out of the training room and back towards my office. All of a sudden I heard my name called from the other end of the hall. It was Aaron. Here we go, I thought.

chapter **17**

"What's happening?" asked Aaron.

"I've just held a planning meeting with my staff. You remember I invited you to learn about a process for finding improvements? This is it."

"From what I can see, there's a lot of talking but not a lot of action. I've already made my savings," said Aaron smugly.

"So I heard. I didn't think this was only about cost saving."

"So they say. But they love head trimming around here. I'm just doing what I know they want."

"Doing the right thing doesn't always mean doing what is wanted. There's more than one way to maim this beast – some of them more humane than others," I said righteously.

"Perhaps, but I hope you can catch yours before the time's up."

So did I.

"You haven't seen Amanda have you?" asked Aaron.

No, I hadn't. His question prompted me to realize that in fact I hadn't seen Amanda for a couple of days. It wasn't unusual that we didn't cross paths, as we often worked on opposite shifts. But it was unusual not to see her at all. And she hadn't asked me about covering her staff for her second meeting. That's odd, I thought.

* * *

I left it a few days and then asked Monica to come and see me so we could think about the analysis work.

"There is a real buzz about the place," she said as she approached my desk. "Using the big check-sheet on the wall is a good, simple way of measuring things, but it's also a fantastic way of creating visibility for our project. I've lost count of the number of people from other areas who have asked me what we're up to. I even saw Aaron looking it over this morning. If nothing else, this is certainly making our team feel a bit special – more than Aaron's poor group. Were you aware that he sacked all those people?"

I told her I was, but wanting to avoid sounding judgmental, I asked that we get straight into what we had to do.

"I've been doing some more reading on Six Sigma.

Sounds to me like I'm in for a heavy dose of statistics," enthused Monica. "There must be a lot of mathematics involved here, is there?"

"Yes and no," I said. "The use and presentation of our data is very important, and it would be very hard to see many patterns in our raw data. So we will have to spend some time making up charts and graphs – especially with the spreadsheet data. I guess you already know how to do things like Pareto diagrams, histograms, run charts and scatter diagrams?"

After Monica affirmed this, I went on to remind her that the statistics and analysis would be a means to an end – not an end in themselves. That's one reason, I recalled from conversation with Julia, why *One Bite at a Time* reduces the emphasis on the statistical tools that are so strongly emphasized in the Six Sigma literature. "With the limited time we have, and the fact that you still need to do your normal job, we'll start with the simplest and easiest analysis – things like histograms – and then if necessary you can use more complex tools later on."

"No problem. Leave me to it," said Monica, and off she went.

I turned my attention to tracking down Amanda. She hadn't answered any of my numerous calls, nor replied to any emails. Apart from my obvious concern for her, I was worried that her project would be falling behind. Her team didn't know what was going on. On top of that, it was now only a week until we were due to meet with Julia again.

* * *

"So what does the analysis show us?" I asked Monica the next Wednesday.

Monica showed me a number of smart-looking charts. Happily, she had avoided temptation and managed to keep the charts simple, with each focusing on only one analysis 'story'. It was rapidly clear that the measurement and analysis work had been worthwhile. It confirmed that we did, indeed, have a problem. Category A claims were taking eight days, on average – much longer than we had promised in our advertising only last year. The interruptions issue was much smaller than had been expected; clearly the hassle of these interruptions had increased their perceived frequency. Escalated calls due to exceptions were also less frequent than we had expected but, on the other hand, the faxes were a mess. Almost half of them ended up having pages missing or material that was indecipherable.

"The forms issue is particularly interesting," said Monica. "I did some work on that one just after we spoke last week and it didn't take long to work out that customers make mistakes on their forms a lot. But we weren't really collecting enough detail. It occurred to me that unless we understood which sections of the form were being incorrectly completed more often, we wouldn't be able to do much with the information. Some of us talked about this and we decided to create a separate sheet of flip-chart paper for that issue only. We drew a large, basic version of the form on it and when an error was made, people were able to tick the area on the form where the mistake had been made. We were able to track down the exact areas causing the most problems." Monica produced another set of charts showing her results.

I was again left to reflect on how giving the staff a bit more latitude had inspired a much greater level of initiative. I was also quietly amused when I remembered that, during the consultants' involvement previously, there had been real resistance by the team to having their work measured. But now, on their own project, they were quite happy to measure themselves.

"So, having finished the measurement and analysis, we must be finally ready to choose something to *do*," said Monica anxiously. "Everyone is very keen to get 'fixing'."

"We'll meet early next week and make our plans," I assured her. With that my phone rang and Monica left me to answer it.

"Amanda! Where have you been?" I blurted into the handset.

chapter **18**

Julia walked into my apartment the next Saturday afternoon. "I haven't heard from you, so I assume that means that things have gone well …" She cut herself off as she saw the frown on my face. "Perhaps not. What's up now?"

The doorbell rang. I was glad for the interruption because I didn't really know what to say. To my surprise, though, it was Amanda.

"Well at least you're looking positive," said Julia. "Grumpy here looks like he's still carrying the planet on his shoulders."

"I've just come out of our second workshop this morning," said Amanda cheerfully. "I managed to get everyone in – and on a Saturday."

"So, spill the beans. How did it go?" asked Julia.

"Very well. The cause and effect diagram worked particularly well. It isn't hard to use, is it? Apart from helping us to identify root causes, it gave us a much better understanding of the problem and the way all the causes can be linked. I ended up asking my team to vote so that we could narrow the causes down to what we felt were the 'most likely'. The only stipulation was that votes had to be applied to the deeper root causes – not to the first-level ones."

"That's a great idea," enthused Julia. "I wish I'd thought of that. We just did it by consensus but I was a bit concerned that this was taking the 'simple' thing a bit too far and risked the quieter members not having enough say. So what about measurement? You haven't had a chance to do any of that have you?"

Looking across at me a little guiltily, Amanda finally explained her absence. Her fiancé had been very ill for a couple of days – so ill that he had been hospitalized. Amanda had told the boss, who was out of town, but he hadn't bothered to advise anyone at the office.

"You're lucky you have a team working for you who are so self-reliant," Julia commented.

Amanda agreed. Then she went on to explain that the two days spent at her fiancé's bedside had got her thinking about her priorities. She had resolved then and there that the stress associated with her job wasn't worth it and that she would just pull the plug and not come back. On the pretence that her fiancé was still gravely ill, she had stayed at home and started thinking about finding a new job.

This much I knew already, as she had brought me up to date on the phone. It was the next part of Amanda's story that was a surprise. Only two days ago, one of Amanda's team had paid her an unexpected visit. This staff member had told her how anxious the team had become. She had also told Amanda about all the action happening in my team and how positive the culture of the team was becoming. She learnt about how down on everything Aaron's team had become, too.

At the last minute, Amanda had had a change of heart. She couldn't stand the fact that her team were closer in mood to Aaron's than mine. So, over the phone, she had quickly had her people pull together and organize their second meeting for the Saturday – this very morning.

"I know we're behind," she said as she finished her story, "but we think we can catch up. We'll have less time for making improvement, but we still think, with eight weeks to go, that we can make a difference."

"Phew! You don't do your traumas by halves, do you?" said Julia. "But you know what, I think you'll be okay. It's one of the strengths of *One Bite at a Time* that even with a disruption like this a lot can still be done. A number of people who did the program with me missed a couple of weeks due to holidays, and they still managed to complete a good project."

Amongst all this, my head was still spinning with Amanda's latest revelations. Ultimately, of course, I was just glad she'd decided to stick it out.

"Well, with your second meeting hot out of the oven," Julia said to Amanda, "we'd better turn our attention to Improve and Control."

"Not before I make afternoon tea," I said, heading for the kitchen. "I'm going to exceed my customers' expectations this time."

Stage Three:

IMPROVE AND CONTROL

chapter 19

Improve

"So *finally* we get to fix our problem," said Trevor.

"Yes," I said with a smile. "And we still have six weeks to go, so it's not all bad, is it? The question is, having been through those first three stages – Define, Measure and Analyze – do you agree that there was value in doing them?"

For me, with the benefit of hindsight, it all seemed like common sense. 'Organized common sense', as Bill Smith had put it. In fact it seemed crazy to think that anyone wouldn't use something like this approach to solve *all* their productivity and quality problems. A few comments from my team indicated that they were feeling the same way. Our early skepticism had given way as the pieces of Six Sigma and *One Bite at a Time* were falling into place.

An interesting aspect of *One Bite at a Time* was the extent to which it had already had a positive impact on the general culture of my area. In particular, I was enjoying the way people seemed willing to take initiative again, where previously they had felt constrained by bureaucracy. It was as though they needed permission to see the 'too easy' problems in that light, where previously they saw everything as 'too hard'.

But it was time to move on with some action.

"Now, although the preparation has been worthwhile, it should be obvious that it is no replacement for actually doing something – for fixing our problem, as Trevor is so keen to do," I said with a grin.

"Remember when we moved offices a few years ago? Some of you helped in the planning of that. The way I see it, conducting the Improve stage of our *One Bite at a Time* project shouldn't really be any different. Once again it's not that Six Sigma offers us any magic to help get things done – it just fits the normal tools for getting things done into a robust structure."

"So it won't be long before you're talking about discipline again, will it?" asked Trevor knowingly.

"Got it in one. The key difference between successfully taking action or not usually boils down to discipline rather than process. That's why deadlines work so well." I was all too well aware of my own weakness in this area. Sometimes I wondered if I would ever achieve anything without a deadline, and the discipline that it forced on me.

For the sake of those who hadn't been around for the office move, I explained what I'd said many times during the project. Because the building was to be demolished on a specific date, we couldn't use the usual excuses of being busy to put moving tasks off. We just *had* to do them. So we did.

Julia had told me how important the three-month deadline had been for her project. The cut-off date for the presentation had created the necessary sense of urgency for all those involved to apply the discipline they needed to get things done. Of course, we didn't need a false deadline in that way. We had a real one. Show our improvements or, for some of us at least, lose our jobs. I had no real concerns about motivation or discipline here.

"So we need to use the deadline to create urgency and maintain our momentum," said someone.

"That's right," I agreed. "We have about six weeks for this Improve stage – about half of our program. If we're not careful, we could still let day-to-day urgent tasks take up most of our working hours until the last minute. Not a good idea."

"But surely those everyday tasks are important – it's not as if we can shut down our whole department for six weeks," said Monica.

"You're absolutely right," I said. "It's all about finding the right balance. It's just that the really important things, like trying to improve our processes, usually aren't all that *urgent*. It doesn't really matter if you work on it today or the next day – but it *does* matter if you never get to work on it at all. That's what can happen when the smaller but more urgent things keep filling up our days.

"As long as we keep some focus on our project during the early and middle part of the Improve stage, we should be fine. All we need to do is include the project as an agenda item in our weekly team meeting. That way we can make sure that everyone is on track to complete their allocated tasks and that intermediate deadlines are being met. Each of us needs to be disciplined about doing our bit and, together, we need to be disciplined about following up in that way."

"How will we know who needs to do what?" asked someone.

"The first thing we'll do, which we'll start in this meeting, is break the task into manageable steps. For example, we know we have to draft a new claim form based on what we learnt about how customers keep filling the current one in incorrectly. That will involve a few steps: someone to work out what has to go on the form and what can be left off, someone to design an alternative, someone else to test the alternative, and so on. For each of our mini-projects, we'll need to identify the individual tasks involved and you'll either volunteer for them – or I'll delegate them."

Delegation was something I'd had a lot of trouble with early in my supervisory career. I knew that often I had tried to do too much myself. I'd long since learnt that while delegating a task meant it might not be done exactly as I would do it, nor even, occasionally, as well as I might have, it was ultimately the only way that my team members would learn to take on more responsibility. Here, particularly as the team were already taking more initiative, it would be even more important to avoid micro-managing and allow my staff to take responsibility for how they achieved their own tasks.

"What if this thing ends up being much bigger than we expect?" asked Trevor.

"Well there's one thing we can't do," I said, "and that is apply for an extension. I guess we would potentially look to lower our sights, if we really had to. For example, if our target processing time of two days was not achievable in the time available, we might aim for a smaller improvement – let's say four days – and then present a plan for further improvements. While we need to present numbers, the management group are essentially looking for evidence that we can make serious productivity improvements. I'm sure, if the trends are in the right direction, that we'll be able to satisfy them." At least I hoped so. I wasn't really sure, as the boss had never been clear with me. It was, I still thought, one reason why his ultimatum had been so unfair. But for the moment I kept these thoughts to myself.

Finally the questions ceased and we turned our attention to planning our improvements. This ended up being a very straightforward exercise, which I could only attribute to the extent of the preparation we had already done. I couldn't help but see an analogy with house painting: invest in good preparation and the actual painting is easy; skimp on the preparation and the painting is not only difficult, it won't last.

Having clearly identified the highest-impact causes of our problem (and communicated them to the team with Monica's simple but smart charts), we were able to hone in on those causes most worthy of addressing. We brainstormed potential solutions to each of them and came up with about half a dozen 'to-dos' for each. We then ranked those solutions based on how easy they would be to complete, and how much relative impact they would have on our processing delay problem.

Having done that, we now had a dozen mini-projects to complete. Julia had suggested that instead of trying to identify all the necessary tasks for each of these mini-projects, we should only identify the first two or three steps for each. That was a great idea. It really took the pressure off. And it made so much sense. Why plan every minute step when something might change after doing the first couple?

The main challenge we faced was making sure each task was small enough. We had defined a task as an action that could be done by one person in one sitting. It took some disciplined thinking and questioning to get all the tasks that small. But again, it was clearly going to be a worthwhile approach because it would leave very little room for excuses on the part of those allocated a job. If it was all down to the individual with their name against it, they couldn't blame anyone else for not finishing what they had committed to.

Within a couple of hours we had wrapped it up. And most people left the room with at least one task to do.

"Still talking are you?" Aaron came into the training room the moment after the last of my team left. I got the distinct impression he had been eavesdropping, but I decided against challenging him on that. I wasn't going to let him burst today's bubble. I even found it in me to tell him what we had been doing, in some detail, without feeling too smug.

"It's all very exciting, isn't it?" he said haughtily when

I'd finished. Even if we had been able to convince Aaron to follow the *One Bite at a Time* approach at the outset, I wondered now if he would have had the patience to see it through. It occurred to me that nothing would be worse than half doing a *One Bite* project and then panicking, giving up, and just taking the quickest, most obvious way out. Then I remembered that that was exactly what I had wanted to do.

"What's so funny?" asked Aaron when he saw me smile.

"Nothing, Aaron."

At that moment Amanda rushed into the room, looking very flustered. "Have you heard? We've had two weeks cut off our timeline."

So much for my bubble.

"The boss pulled me into his office," Amanda continued, "to tell me that some bigwig from head office will be in town in a month and he wants him to be able to see our presentations. I haven't even had my third meeting yet."

"No problem," said Aaron with a smirk. "I could address him tomorrow if needed. I told you it was better to act sooner rather than later." And with that comment hanging, he left the room.

Amanda and I gathered our thoughts. The team won't like this, I thought. But I felt confident they would focus quickly on the new deadline and just work more intently on meeting it. In the meantime, I could set to work on some slides for the presentation. Given we'd been asked to present our project as a whole – not just the results – I knew we already had a good story to tell. All of a sudden I found myself surprised at how calm I was feeling.

Then I remembered poor Amanda. She had taken a seat nearby and was deep in thought. It was clear her thoughts were nowhere near as reasoned or rational as mine. I could almost see the mental knots she was tying herself up in.

"I give up," she exclaimed finally. "I really don't need this."

chapter 20

Control

I'd like to be able to say that I maintained my rational mode of thinking until the end of the project. But I can't. My brain seemed to relish that night's sleep as an opportunity to flush out all my previous concerns. I tossed and turned as one potential disaster after another was brought forth. By morning I was shattered – and worried.

Once again I was going to have to call in the reinforcements. And that meant Julia. The only problem was, I couldn't track her down. For two days I left messages and sent emails but to no avail. She'd dropped into the same communication vacuum Amanda had been in a couple of weeks before. I was starting to wonder if it was me.

I distracted myself by helping Amanda get her team together for their Improve meeting and, in the end, I helped her run it. It wasn't until the end of this meeting, with some tasks planned and delegated, that she started to regain her composure. She was still an awfully long way away from her old, cheerful and unflappable self, though.

As for my own staff, a large group of them were admirably unfazed by the news of the shortened timeline. Their resilience was so great they couldn't help drag the remainder along in their wake.

But none of this really eased the concerns I was harboring. They spilled over when, finally, Julia called me at home one evening. I didn't give her a chance to explain her disappearance.

"This could be a complete mess," I said anxiously. "We're going to run out of time. We might only have half a result to present. And Aaron – he'll be the shining light again. The big hero, just by taking the easy way out. And I realize we haven't looked at Control yet. I really think we'll have to leave that until later ..."

"No, no, no, no, *NO*," interrupted Julia. "Control is your secret weapon. When you stand up to talk to these senior managers, do you think they're going to be impressed by short-term wins that are unlikely to be sustained?"

"I guess not. After all, if our gains can't be sustained, we will probably end up back here again next year."

"That's right. Now, how sustainable do you think Aaron's improvements are going to be?"

I started to see where Julia was heading. "Not very –

at least not on their own. It's one thing to reduce the head count. But unless the rest of his team find ways of working more effectively, they'll all just be working harder to cover the extra workload. Eventually something will have to give." I was thoughtful for a moment. "So … if we can demonstrate that we've put Control into place so that our improvements will stick, our presentation will have a lot more substance, won't it?"

"You got it," said Julia. "Even if you've only just started your improvements and don't have many results yet, if you have a plan to maintain them, you'll be looking good."

* * *

The next day I pulled my group together for a quick meeting.

"You're doing a great job," I said, "but we need to cover one other area: Control. This will ensure that whatever improvements we make are maintained. This is an area where our project differs from the office move we talked about last time."

"Yes," interrupted Trevor with a laugh. "Control in that case was easy: our old building had been knocked down so there was no turning back."

"Some of our improvements involve changes to procedures," I went on. "For example, you're developing a different way of handling the faxes. It's going to take quite a lot of discipline from everyone involved for the new procedures to stick, at least until new habits form. What would happen if we stopped doing the new process? The fax problem would quickly get worse and we'd be back to square one. And all your efforts in planning and implementing the change would have been wasted. Importantly, it's not the short term we need to worry about with Control. In the short term the 'new way' will be front of mind and you'll all be motivated to maintain the new systems. But in six or 12 months? All sorts of new things will be competing for our immediate focus and if we're not careful, the old problems could gradually reappear."

"What can we do to stop that happening?" asked somebody.

"A friend of mine gave me this phrase recently and it really helped me to understand the essence of Control: 'What gets measured, gets done'."

"Not measurement again," came a groaned reply. "Haven't we done enough of that."

"Well, no. I'm afraid we haven't," I said, feeling a little guilty. This was more or less what I had said to Julia during a similar conversation the night before. I echoed what she had said to me. "We have to get past seeing measurement as a one-off chore. It has to become an integrated part of our everyday work. Just as it is in all successful businesses. Do you remember what we measured during the Measurement stage?"

After a few attempted answers, which focused on detail, I managed to get the response I was looking for. We had measured two things. First, the size of the problem, both to make sure it really was worth fixing and to provide us with a baseline so we could track any improvements. Secondly, we had measured some potential causes to work out which ones were having a significant impact on the problem.

"Well the good news is we don't have to keep doing all that measurement. At a minimum, all we need to keep measuring is the problem – our speed of processing Category A claims."

"And the system can do that for us," called out Monica.

"Exactly. Though we will need to do the analysis and post the results regularly so everyone can see them," I said. "That way we'll quickly see if we start slipping backwards. If those measurements ever indicate that things are going bad, we can get in and re-measure the causes, just as we did during the project, and make the necessary adjustments. Monica, if you can keep producing those charts, I'll make sure we refer to them at each weekly meeting."

Monica nodded. "That will be another change, though, won't it? At the moment we're measuring the problem every day. Now we will be changing to a weekly measurement."

"That's right," I said. "If we don't intend to react to the numbers every day, we won't need to measure them every day."

"So we don't need to do that crazy shareholder thing?" asked Trevor. "You know – checking stock prices every 20 minutes even though you have no intention of selling. What happens in between our weekly measurements won't really be relevant.

"What I don't get," Trevor went on, "is why we're talking about this now. You said this Control stuff happens in the months after the project. We have heaps to do – couldn't it have waited?"

"I thought the same thing," I said. I relayed my conversation with Julia about the importance of having Control in place from the outset, and certainly before the presentation.

"And in any case," I continued, "we're all working so hard leading up to this presentation, how do you think we're going to feel after it finally happens?"

"Relieved," said a voice from the back.

"And anxious to catch up on all those unanswered emails and phone calls," said someone else.

"Exactly," I said. "So can you see how easy it would be to let things slip? It would be very easy to mentally tick off our project as done and forget that things need to be maintained. If we put our Control into place *before* the presentation, we won't let that happen."

There was general agreement on this point.

"Okay everyone," said Trevor, taking the lead. "We have only three weeks left until P Day. Let's get back to work."

I was left to reflect on the deeper change that was happening in my area. Where my team – and particularly 'old-timers' like Trevor – had previously resisted change, they were now fierce advocates for it. It seemed to me that the reason for this was no more complicated than the fact that they had been involved all the way through. It was *their* change they were making, not someone else's.

I went out to catch up with Amanda, hoping that her team were seeing things as positively as mine.

The

PRESENTATION

chapter 21

Julia was running late for our last get together. She had agreed to one more afternoon with Amanda and me, to help us prepare our presentations.

"We've got lots to tell," Amanda said while we waited, "but only a 20-minute slot to tell it in. I'm a bit worried about how we'll fit it all in."

I smiled at this change of circumstance. Amanda had done a brilliant job in the last few weeks of her project. Despite the late start and her virtual breakdown when the presentation was brought forward, she had pulled her team together through the Improve stage. They had also implemented a simple but powerful Control mechanism that would form the basis for their presentation as it showed how much they had improved their problem – in only the first three weeks.

I was feeling similarly pressed in terms of fitting our story into only 20 minutes. What's more, because we had such a good story to tell, nearly all my team wanted a part of the presentation action. That only gave each person about two minutes. I still had to work that out, but there was an upside. It looked as though I wouldn't have to face my own presentation demons, at least not for now.

Telling our stories succinctly was the first issue we grilled Julia on when she arrived.

"To keep our presentation flowing," said Julia, "we used a structure that closely followed the overall *One Bite at a Time* program. First we ..."

"Hang on ... can I try guessing your presentation outline?" I offered.

Julia nodded knowingly and I grabbed a pen and fresh sheet of paper.

"Very good." Julia seemed pleased that I was able to so quickly rattle off the five steps of the Six Sigma DMAIC process. "Essentially, that's what we did – with only a few additions. First, I was aware that not everyone in the room knew exactly what our team's role was. So instead of starting with our problem I gave them a quick overview of the team. Secondly, I wanted to make sure everyone heard about our 'quick wins' too, so we had a slide about that.

"Then I thought about the fact that there would be a lot of managers there – and you know what they always want to hear, don't you?"

"The bottom line?" I ventured.

"Exactly. Not necessarily in dollar terms, but they were keen to know what impact the problem was having on the business and what the benefits of our improvements had been so far and would be in future. So I included a specific 'Benefits Summary' slide after the process.

"And finally I spoke for a few minutes about what my team and I had learnt during the program. I think that was important because in my view, that's where the organization got the real value. Yes, we delivered some improvements as part of this project, but we now had the *capacity* to repeat the process over and over again. I wanted to make it clear that there was potential for much larger projects that could deliver much larger results."

Presentation Outline

1. About our team
2. Definition of our problem and goal
3. Measure and Analysis of the problem and its likely causes
4. Improvements that were made
5. Control: how the gains will be sustained
6. Additional 'Quick Wins'
7. Benefits summary
8. Learnings

"I guess we can make that point too," said Amanda, "though I think their main interest will be on the *now* at this meeting."

I agreed, but added, "They also want to be assured that we will continue to be competitive and find ways to improve. So the ability to repeat the process has to be a positive thing."

Julia corrected my original outline to include the extra sections she had talked about.

"There's still a lot to get through in 20 minutes," I commented.

"That's true," said Julia, "which is why it's really important that you do plenty of preparation. You need to prepare your presentation and then rehearse it as often as you can. Some of your people will want to waffle – practice will give you the chance to get them under control *before* the main presentation. You don't want to be physically dragging them off on the day."

"How did you prepare for it?" asked Amanda.

"About a week before the presentation," Julia explained, "we had a fourth training session that focused on exactly that. We had each drafted what we wanted to say and we did a quick run-through first up. It was interesting to see how the other teams were coming along and I got some really useful feedback from the other team leaders and the facilitators."

"Such as …?" I wondered out loud.

"Well, for me it was mainly that most of us spoke too quickly – instead of 20 minutes, we only took 12. Probably just nerves. The other good feedback was that our slides were far too cluttered. The graphs needed to be made bigger and clearer, each making one or two points only. We had to avoid the temptation to try and tell *everything* in one slide."

I was suddenly glad that Monica had already proved herself capable of producing simple, easy-to-understand charts.

"Overall, I'm sure that the practice and feedback made a huge difference to our final presentation," Julia said finally. With that she pulled out her computer and for the rest of the afternoon took us through her own presentation and those of some of her colleagues. I was surprised how different the presentations were even though each one used the same DMAIC process.

* * *

After Julia had left, Amanda and I spent some time discussing what was to come. The strange thing was we still didn't really know whether we were on the right track. We didn't know how the managers would compare our thorough approach (as we saw it) with Aaron's quick-and-dirty cost cutting. And if they did prefer one approach over another, we had no idea whether they intended to 'let go' any of us, as they would call it. And if so, how they would choose. It all felt very strange and I couldn't help but be envious of Julia's much more positive situation – a situation in which the *One Bite at a Time* approach had been seen as an opportunity for team development and growth as much as for productivity and quality improvements.

chapter 22

All too quickly the big day arrived. There was a real buzz around our office. My team had gone to fantastic lengths to make this special. Hair had been done. Clothes were all freshly pressed. Shoes that hadn't been shined for a good while glistened. I felt as though I'd walked onto a naval parade ground.

All for 20 minutes of glory, I smiled to myself.

The boss's assistant had allocated times to us. Aaron was to go first, followed by Amanda and then me. The three of us were to be present in the room all the time; as space was tight, our teams could come in only for their own presentations.

I felt remarkably calm. I wasn't sure if that was because I was off the hook in terms of presenting, or simply because I had developed a quiet confidence that we would come through this unscathed. Deep down, though, there was still plenty of uncertainty, and it wasn't helped when I walked into the meeting room and saw the serious faces of about 10 senior managers dressed in almost uniform grey suits - even the two women amongst them. My boss introduced us to everyone. Some of the managers I knew from other branches and a couple from head office. The 'bigwig' Amanda had referred to was actually the CEO, who was one of the group I knew already. Three or four were strangers to me.

We took our seats. I winked at Amanda and she smiled back. She seemed to share my confidence.

The session started with the boss explaining the exercise he had set us. Of course, as was his way, he made it all sound like a very positive initiative on his part. It was all about enhancing productivity, increasing shareholder value and the rest. There was no mention of increasing workloads or potential downsizing.

Aaron stood up. On his own. None of his team were with him, which, on reflection, didn't surprise me. He went straight to the numbers and showed various slides with charts showing productivity rates and costs. His mastery of corporate-speak was as good as you will hear anywhere.

About 10 minutes in, he was interrupted. "So what have you actually done?" asked the CEO bluntly. "And what do you plan to do?"

Aaron paused, taken aback. Amanda and I exchanged glances.

It seemed to take some time for Aaron to compose himself. He flicked past his next half-dozen slides, finally resting on one that showed, over time, the staffing levels for his department and the effective processing cost per claim. Both took a quantum step down at the point where he had laid off three staff. He explained the chart then quickly finished off, talking about productivity gains as the staff adjusted to their new, heavier workload.

At the end of his presentation, Aaron was questioned about his future plans. It was a cause of some relief to me that the CEO focused almost exclusively on how sustainable Aaron thought his changes were.

And so to Amanda's group. It was striking how much the air in the room seemed to lighten as four of her staff filed in, brimming with a mixture of nervousness, enthusiasm and pride.

The presentation was nowhere near as polished as Aaron's had been, but it was clear that it was lifting the spirits of the executives. By the end of the presentation, over half of them had replaced their scowls with smiles. My confidence grew.

Finally, my own team came through the door. They had worked out together that 10 presenters in 20 minutes would be excessive and had eventually whittled the group down to just five. The others were all here too, however, offering moral support.

When it came to their presentation, they had practiced it so often that it was almost professional in its style. But, more importantly, there was an abundance of substance. I couldn't have been more proud of their efforts. They explained their measurements clearly, how they had identified likely causes and what they had implemented to date. They explained the controls they had put into place, their quick wins, and the benefits to the company. The benefits were much greater than we had expected they would be. It was surprising how a little focus could find such significant financial rewards for the business.

I stood up with them at the end to help with questions. Most centered around the individuals' experiences – much less on the results they had produced. Which surprised me. I could tell the management team were impressed by what we'd done and also by the professionalism of this group of 'front-liners'. I don't think they believed we had it in us. I was pretty sure my boss didn't.

And then it was all over. My team, plus Aaron, Amanda and I, all left the grey suits to discuss what they'd heard. On the way out I caught the eye of my boss, who gave me a smile and a nod. First smile I've had from him for a long time, I thought.

I told my team we'd meet up the street for a celebratory drink at the end of the day. They went off, chattering busily. I turned around to speak to Aaron, but he had disappeared.

FINALE

chapter 23

The display board in Arrivals sounded like a flock of startled pigeons taking flight. As the new letters settled on the board, I noticed with dismay that the flight was delayed by 40 minutes. Typical.

With time on my hands, I chose a concourse at random and started to slowly walk its length. Like a pedestrian freeway, hundreds of passengers, laden with their carry-on bags, were scurrying backwards and forwards to either catch their plane or to escape the airport by some other means.

As I moved slowly along, I noticed a cleaner pushing a rubbish trolley. She was emptying the bins that lined either side of the concourse. After emptying one bin she moved diagonally across the thoroughfare to the next bin on the other side, zigzagging her way. Along the way she had to avoid the throng of people – and they had to avoid her and her trolley – slowing their stride and moving to one side or the other.

After watching a few minor collisions and countless near misses, I began to think about her process. It was clearly inconveniencing the passengers and also taking the cleaner a long time to move from side to side. Here was a process that could do with some improving. I wondered why she didn't empty all the bins on one side, moving with the crowd – then come back down the other side. I was sure that this cleaner and her colleagues would have been able to think up a solution like this (or perhaps a better one) if only they were given the opportunity.

I soon found myself standing outside one of the many food outlets. A quick snack would help pass the time. The outlet was crammed with customers and clearly a popular choice. After I ordered, I was given a plastic tag with a beeper attached. Instead of my order being called out, I was told, my tag would beep when my food was ready. I knew the order would take some time because of the crowds, but I wasn't in any hurry. However, with this beeper, I no longer had to stand next to the counter waiting – I had some freedom to move around. Furthermore, I am sure this would have saved the counter staff the time and hassle of trying to let their customers know when their meals were ready.

Here was a process that was clearly working. They had found a solution that was a win-win-win for their customers, the staff and the business as a whole.

Minutes later, as I was eating, I started musing over what I'd just seen: emptying bins and serving food.

Everywhere I went lately, I was seeing interconnected processes and putting myself in the customers' shoes – wondering what could be done to improve their experience. Of course, that is what I had been doing at work in a very structured way. But more and more I was finding that these principles really did apply everywhere.

Outside the gate, the growing crowd advertised the impending arrival of another flight. A single line of disembarking passengers started making their way through the crowd. Some were pausing, looking expectantly for a familiar face. Others were striding purposefully towards the exit, obviously not expecting any company.

Julia appeared through the doorway, one of the latter group. With her eyes straight ahead, she moved into the main flow of the concourse.

I moved up behind her and lightly tapped her on her shoulder. She turned around. For a second she was startled, but then broke into a broad smile and gave me a hug.

"What a fantastic surprise!" she said. "I had no idea you'd be here. In fact, how *did* you know I'd be on this flight?"

I smiled, pleased that my little surprise had held up. "I rang your home a few days ago and spoke to Mark.

He told me you were away and would be coming back today. He gave me your flight details and agreed to keep it a secret. Hope you don't mind?"

"Not at all; it's good to see you. And you look great. I assume this is good news then?"

"It certainly is," I laughed.

As we waited at the baggage carousel, I began telling Julia all about our presentations and what had happened since.

"So your job is safe. And so is Amanda's. That's fantastic," said Julia when I'd explained what I'd been told by the boss only a couple of days before. "What about that other person – what was his name again?"

"Aaron. Well, funnily enough, he's safe too. But he's been instructed to take his team through a *One Bite at a Time* project. I'm to help him, as I'm the resident expert all of a sudden."

"So no one has been sacked?"

I explained that the three people Aaron had laid off wouldn't be coming back. The company couldn't afford to reverse a decision like that, having made it. And they still expected the productivity gains we were making to reflect in the bottom line somewhere. But other than that, all was well.

"In fact the CEO was so impressed by our teams' presentations that he's decided to roll the program out across all the other departments in our division."

"Wow! That's terrific," said Julia.

"And, best of all, they've asked me to play a central role in the rollout. I'm to coordinate the whole program."

"Congratulations," she smiled. "And to think that only a couple of months ago we were talking about the promotional opportunities that might come from doing this thing properly. So what are your plans? Tell me all about them."

I was about to launch into a detailed description when I looked up to see an animated figure walking hurriedly toward us.

"Sorry I'm late," puffed Amanda. It was the old Amanda – the smiling Amanda with the infectious enthusiasm. It's great to have you back, I thought to myself. Julia and Amanda embraced like old friends.

"Come on," I said as Julia turned and picked her bag off the carousel. "Dinner is on me: *One Bite at a Time!*"

Epilogue

To give credit where it is due, Aaron gave his *One Bite at a Time* project a real go. I realized later that it wasn't that he didn't like new ideas, he simply didn't like taking risks. As soon as he saw the *One Bite* approach could work, he was willing to give it a try.

A few weeks after his first project presentation, I was at his desk asking him when the next would start.

"You're joking, aren't you?" he said. "Surely we've finished now? I thought that having put Control into place, it would all be over."

"That project might be over," I said, "but to stop at this point would be a disservice to all the time and effort you've put in so far. *One Bite at a Time* doesn't mean taking only one bite. It means taking many – but one at a time. In fact, the process should become part of our everyday work. That's how we can bed down the real cultural change we've already started to see around here."

"So having addressed one problem, we need to get started on another ... and then another," he said. "But surely we'll eventually run out of problems to fix. What then?"

I laughed. "Somehow, I don't think I'll live to see that day. Look at my team. We initially identified three 'just right' problems to be fixed. At the moment, we're halfway through the last of these. After that, we can start working on some of our 'too hard' problems. By then, those probably won't seem so hard after all, particular as other departments will have learnt the *One Bite at a Time* approach too so there'll be scope to do joint projects. And after we've finished those we could start pushing ourselves even harder."

I explained that as we reduced or eliminated one set of problems, other smaller problems would present themselves. We had really started on an ongoing process of continual improvement.

"I can see what you're saying," said Aaron. "But how will a program like this survive the usual changes of direction they love to impose around here. How can we prevent it falling victim to the next fad that comes along?"

It was a good question. "I guess it will need a strong commitment from those of us who believe it works. Remember, Amanda and I were able to do our first projects using our own initiative – independent of all the other code-named projects going on around us. I can't see any reason why, if we're determined enough, we can't keep doing that."

Aaron nodded as he opened his desk drawer and took out a folder. He quickly found the page he was looking for and spent a moment scanning the list.

"That's right. I remember now," he said, suddenly animated. "During our first Define meeting, there were two 'just right' problems our team really wanted to do. I had quite a bit of trouble deciding between them. I'm sure my team will be keen to get started on the one we didn't end up choosing that time, if I give them the chance."

As I walked back to my desk I knew that giving them the chance was all it would take. Aaron's team had tasted success with their first project and they now had the skills to run another one with very little help from me. I was already looking forward to his next presentation in three months time.

David Brewster and Gary Calwell originally worked together over 15 years ago teaching 16 year-olds how to team together to climb through a spider's web and fly across an imaginary river. Both are experienced consultants and educators. Their combined careers have encompassed research, quality management, operations management, recruitment, training and training development, documentation and information technology. David and Gary have worked in a broad range of industries including telecommunications, banking and finance, health care, manufacturing, mining, primary production, publishing and utilities. Both live in Melbourne, Australia.

David Brewster's background includes ten years in 'hands-on' management roles and ten years working as a consultant and educator. David is an accomplished speaker and facilitator. He has run workshops and seminars with most of his clients as well as presenting to a number of industry group conferences. He is the current President of the National Speakers' Association of Australia (Victoria Chapter). David is qualified with a First-Class Honors Degree in Applied Science and a Graduate Diploma in Information Systems. David is the author of *Success with Simplicity: Take Management Back to Basics*.

Gary Calwell has been the principal of his own consulting firm since 1995. As an instructional designer, Gary has developed system training to support in-house software development and business training such as customer service, train-the-trainer, and quality. He has also managed many documentation projects to support a range of change initiatives. Gary has facilitated interactive workshops in these areas and also presented to larger audiences at local and national conferences. Gary is qualified with a Bachelors Degree in Engineering and a Graduate Diploma in Human Resources Development.

FOR FURTHER ASSISTANCE

One Bite at a Time Field Guide

The *One Bite at a Time Field Guide* takes you step-by-step through the approach described in this book. The Field Guide:

- explains the DMAIC process in detail,
- shows you how to conduct the workshops you'll need to run with your staff, and
- teaches you how to use the various tools.

The *One Bite at a Time Field Guide* has been compiled from materials successfully used by scores of team leaders, supervisors and managers in a range of industry settings.

For more information, or to order your copy, visit www.obaatime.com.

One Bite at a Time Licensing Opportunities

If you're a consultant, business coach, training professional or human resources manager and you'd like to use the *One Bite at a Time* approach with your clients or staff, we can provide you with all the materials and support you need to do so.

For more information visit www.obaatime.com.

One Bite at a Time Facilitation

Our keynote speeches, seminars and workshops will help you convince others of the benefits of the *One Bite at a Time* approach. For more information on how we can help you directly, visit www.diyresults.com.